POLITICAL THEORY AND INTERNATIONAL AFFAIRS

POLITICAL THEORY
AND
INTERNATIONAL AFFAIRS

Hans J. Morgenthau on Aristotle's
The Politics

Edited by
ANTHONY F. LANG, JR.

Foreword by
JOEL H. ROSENTHAL

Humanistic Perspectives on International Relations
Cathal J. Nolan, Series Editor

PRAEGER

**Westport, Connecticut
London**

Library of Congress Cataloging-in-Publication Data

Morgenthau, Hans Joachim, 1904–
  Political theory and international affairs : Hans J. Morgenthau on Aristotle's The Politics / edited by Anthony F. Lang, Jr.
    p. cm.—(Humanistic perspectives on international relations, ISSN 1535–0363)
    Includes bibliographical references and index.
    ISBN 0–275–98025–1 (alk. paper)—ISBN 0–275–98030–8 (pbk : alk. paper)   1. Aristotle.
Politics.   2. Aristotle—Contributions in political science.   3. World politics.   I. Lang, Anthony F.,
1968–   II. Title.   III. Series.
JC71.A7M667   2004
320'.01'1—dc22   2004014773

British Library Cataloguing in Publication Data is available.

Library of Congress Catalog Card Number: 2004014773
ISBN: 0–275–98025–1
      0–275–98030–8 (pbk.)
ISSN: 1535–0363

First published in 2004

Praeger Publishers, 88 Post Road West, Westport, CT 06881
An imprint of Greenwood Publishing Group, Inc.
www.praeger.com

Printed in the United States of America

∞™

The paper used in this book complies with the
Permanent Paper Standard issued by the National
Information Standards Organization (Z39.48–1984).

10 9 8 7 6 5 4 3 2 1

Contents

Series Foreword

Cathal J. Nolan

International relations is a thoroughly humanistic subject. All its actors are human beings, or they are institutions and organizations built and controlled by human intention and maintained by daily decision making. Individual states, which emerged as the most powerful and decisive actors on the world stage over the past 350 years, are not reified constructs with an independent will or social reality beyond human ken or volition. Properly regarded, they are wholly human constructs. All states are designed for, and are bent to, the realization of goals and aspirations of human communities. That is true whether those ambitions are good or evil, spiritual or material, personal or dynastic, or represent ethnic, national, or emerging cosmopolitan identities. So, too, is the international society of states a human construct, replete with its tangled labyrinth of international organizations, an expansive system of international law which creates binding obligations across frontiers, ancient norms of diplomacy and ritualized protocol, webs of economic, social, and cultural interaction, and a venerable penchant for disorder, discord, and war.

Immanuel Kant observed with acute accuracy, "Out of the crooked timbre of Humanity, no straight thing was ever made." The endless drama of human affairs thus gives rise to motley events, decisions, and complex causal chains. At the international level, too, we encounter the foibles of human beings as individuals and in the aggregate, and come upon a mix of the rational and irrational in human motivation. All that makes formal "modeling" of international politics a virtual impossibility—a fact which is itself a source of deep frustration to idealistic reformers and social scientists alike. On the other hand, precisely because international relations is so deeply humanistic a subject, it is a rich realm for the exercise of broad political and moral judgment. It is a natural arena for serious ethical reflection by and about those who frame foreign policies and practice statecraft. It

is proper for scholars and informed citizens to praise or censure leadership decisions and actions. In short, as in all realms of human endeavor, moral judgment is
not only implicit in every decision or action (or inaction) taken in international relations, it is a core duty of leadership, an apt function of scholarship, and a basic
requirement for any educated citizenry.

These facts are clear, and even self-evident. At its classical best, political science understood them and therefore drew its questions from the conversation
across time of the great political thinkers, as well as from current policy debates,
to examine both in a rich discourse which was historically and philosophically
aware, even as it was rigorous and well-grounded empirically. In contrast, much
contemporary political science purports to describe and explain international relations through elaboration of objective "laws" of politics or economics, which
entirely overlook its humanistic character. At its modern and postmodern worst,
the discipline is prone to mere methodological preoccupations, striking elaborate
poses about arcane topics, and impenetrable prose. For instance, positivism's
search for a "rational choice" model of human conduct assumes that individuals
are "rational actors" who purposively seek to maximize their interests. In seeking
a universal, deductive theory (broadly modeled on academic economics, where
similar methodologies are employed with little explanatory success), too many
political scientists eschew historical or philosophically informed case study in favor of a crude reduction of all politics to formal models. These usually engage extreme simplifications, couched in an obscurantist terminology, which model what
was already known or is obvious, or they are so generalized that they account for
nothing specific. Over that thin substance is then spread a thick veneer of false
rigor, packaged in mathematical formulas which are, and are intended to be, in-
timidating to the uninitiated. Left out is the fact that most things of lasting importance in human affairs may be explained, not by "rational choices," but by
ideology and ignorance, blundering and stupidity, courage and self-sacrifice, enlightened vision, fanaticism, or blind chance (what Machiavelli called *fortuna*).

Alternately, the "critical theory" school in political science rejects any epistemology holding that reality exists separately from the academic observer and is
therefore objectively knowable to any real degree. All knowledge about international relations instead merely reflects the biases and power interests of the observer (the usual suspects are racial, class, or economic elites). Scholars are
warned against the attempt to achieve objective knowledge of the reality of international relations, which traditionally was the moral and intellectual *raison d'être*
of their profession. Rather than seek to impartially map out, explore, and explain
the international society of states and its complex subsystems and mores—a feat
said to be impossible—scholars are to directly engage and change the world (even
though that, too, ought to be impossible, if they are unable to understand it in the
first place). Too often, this leads to polemical studies which purport to unmask
elites whose pervasive and corrupt power is said to sustain and operate a fatally
unjust international system. There is much intolerance and angry posturing here
as well, in calls for "exposure" of fellow-traveling academic approaches identified

as legitimizing and reinforcing irredeemably illicit power structures. In sum, in its epistemological assertion that all knowledge is radically subjective or merely political, critical theory denies the possibility of objective knowledge or the value of other scholarly traditions.

This series does not support the contention that all significant political action is reducible to rational choice, or that it is impossible to acquire objective knowledge about world affairs. Instead, it promotes a classical, humanistic approach to international relations scholarship. It is dedicated to reviving and furthering the contribution to understanding made by classical studies—by knowledge of history, diplomacy, international law, and philosophy—but it is agnostic regarding the narrow ideology or specific policy conclusions of any given work. It supports scholarly inquiry that is grounded in the historical antecedents of contemporary controversies, and well versed in the great traditions of philosophical inquiry and discourse. The series recognizes that, at its most incisive, international relations is a field of inquiry which cannot be fully understood outside its historical context. The keenest insights into the meaning of economic, legal, cultural, and political facts and issues in contemporary world affairs are always rooted in appreciation that international society is a historical phenomenon, not a theoretical abstraction or a radical departure from prior experience. Hence, the series welcomes interdisciplinary scholarship dealing with the evolution of the governing ideas, norms, and practices of international society. It encourages a dialectic rooted in abiding intellectual, ethical, and practical interests which for centuries have concerned and engaged intelligent men and women as they tried to reconcile the historical emergence of modern states with wider or older notions of political community.

This series is especially interested in scholarly research on the varied effects of differences in power—whether economic, political, or military—on relations among nations and states. The causes of war and the supports of peace, both in general and concerning specific conflicts, remain a core interest of all serious inquiry into international relations. Similarly, there is an enduring need for studies of the core requirements of international order and security, and of international political economy, whether regionally or globally. Also welcome is scholarship that is concerned with the development of international society, both in the formal relations maintained by states and in broader demands for political, economic, social, and cultural justice on the subnational and even individual level. Finally, the series promotes scholarly investigation of the history and changing character and status of international law, into international organization, and any and all other means of decentralized governance which the states have invented to moderate their conflicts and introduce a measure of restraint and equity to the affairs of international society.

Foreword

Most of us who have reached a certain age have some vague memory of reading Aristotle as part of our secondary or undergraduate curriculum. Literature majors were introduced to *The Poetics* and its famous analysis of Greek tragedy. History and political science students were directed to *The Politics*—the philosopher's classic treatise on the formation and maintenance of the state. Regardless of what one read, most readers came away with two basic impressions: First, that Aristotle was a wise man; second, that wise as he was, he was not exactly relevant to our contemporary life. Certainly, for many of us growing up in the turbulent 1960s and 1970s, Aristotle was a marginal figure on our "must read" list. As Hans Morgenthau puts it so bluntly in his opening remarks, "[W]hat has an old guy who lived almost 2,500 years ago to tell us about contemporary political problems?" What indeed.

Of course, Morgenthau's question was rhetorical, and over the course of several semesters he proceeded to answer his own question in profound and compelling ways. In a sense, then, we might think of this book as the long answer to a short question. But what an answer it is!

The reader of this volume is in for an almost magical ride through time—back to the early 1970s when Richard Nixon occupied the White House, when war raged in Vietnam and the antiwar movement raged at home, when women and minorities took their issues to the streets, and when countless Americans wondered what had become of the comfortable status quo that had reigned over our land virtually unbroken since the Second World War. It was during this period—one we now view as a watershed in American social, cultural, and political history—that Hans Morgenthau chose to deliver a series of lectures on Aristotle's *The Politics*, on the work of an "old guy" who lived and died some two and a-half millennia earlier. And it is a testament to the genius of Morgenthau that he did so.

One need only dip into this work to discover that, just as Morgenthau promised in his opening remarks, the concepts and observations of Aristotle were as relevant to the professor's audience in the 1970s as they were to the philosopher's audience in the fourth century BC. Those of us reading this volume today, in the early years of the twenty-first century, quickly come to realize that what Morgenthau says about Aristotle's timeless relevance is no less true about his *own* observations. Indeed, it is almost with a shock that we discover how deeply and immediately Morgenthau's words and thoughts—on the nature of class and government and slavery and women and all the other great issues that these lectures address—relate to our own lives and world today.

As Morgenthau himself says, "[S]ocial and political problems do not change through history," and of course he is correct. Indeed, given the convincing manner in which Morgenthau demonstrates the relevance of Aristotle to the America of the 1970s, it really should not be too surprising to discover that the Morgenthau of the 1970s is so very relevant to the America of the new millennium. For nearly a century, we at the Carnegie Council on Ethics and International Affairs have examined exactly this principle—that there exist certain timeless and ineluctable truths that affect the social and political relationships between and among individuals and, similarly, between and among nation states. This was the vision and mandate of our founder, Andrew Carnegie; and it was the life's work of our friend and mentor, Hans Morgenthau, in whose memory the Carnegie Council has established its annual Hans Morgenthau Memorial Lecture. With this volume, as with the lecture series, we honor that memory.

Joel H. Rosenthal
President, Carnegie Council on Ethics and International Affairs
New York, New York

Acknowledgments

Producing a volume such as this takes many helping hands. Turning Morgenthau's seminars into a published volume was the original idea of Dr. Robert J.
Myers, formerly president of the Carnegie Council on Ethics and International Affairs. He arranged to have Morgenthau's lectures transcribed from audiotapes and
thoroughly edited them. As a student and friend of Hans Morgenthau, Dr. Myers
was the first to see the value in this material. He deserves much of the credit for
helping to make this book a reality.

The current president of the Carnegie Council, Dr. Joel H. Rosenthal, also deserves a great deal of credit. Perhaps because he wrote about Morgenthau in his
own monograph, Joel also saw the value in this material and was instrumental in
encouraging its publication. He also provided the time and encouragement to me
as program officer at the Council in this and in a number of other projects. In
helping to produce this volume, and for all he does to connect the ethical and political, scholars in international affairs owe Joel a great deal.

Others at the Carnegie Council were also instrumental in helping to bring this
volume to fruition. Eva Becker, the vice president of the Carnegie Council, created an environment that enabled me to move this project toward completion.
Deborah Carroll used her computer skills to turn yellowed pages into usable files.
Andrew Reisner, an intern at the Council, read through this material and provided
extremely useful comments on its location in classical political theory. Jenny Ru-
zow, another intern, provided background information on Morgenthau and Aristotle. John Tessitore not only copyedited the text, he added insights and historical
references that rounded out the volume. Liz Leiba of Westchester Book Group
provided additional copyediting, also improving the volume.

The editorial team at Praeger were extremely patient and supportive, especially
Michael Hermann, Hilary Claggett, and Brien McDonald. Cathal Nolan, the editor

of the series in which this volume is located (Humanistic Perspectives on International Relations), has enriched the field of international affairs with his tireless efforts to bring ethical and historical themes to bear on international affairs. Kenneth Thompson, Mitchell Rologas and Benjamin Mollov responded to my queries about Morgenthau and the text in a helpful and timely fashion. Matthew and Susanna, Hans Morgenthau's children, who granted the Council permission to produce this material, were kind enough to donate all the proceeds from its sales to the Carnegie Council's annual Morgenthau lecture series.

My colleagues at Albright College provided insights and a supportive atmosphere in which to complete this project. My wife, Nicki, and my children, Teddy and Beatrice, made life fun during the four years it took to finish this book. My mother, Anna Mae Lang, who passed away as I was finishing this volume, was my first and best teacher. As the mother of five children and grandmother of many more, she understood one of the central insights of both Aristotle and Morgenthau—that a truly wise leader knows when to balance the exercise of power with the pursuit of justice.

Introduction

Anthony F. Lang, Jr.

From 1970 to 1973, Hans J. Morgenthau conducted what appears to have been a series of graduate level seminars on Aristotle's *The Politics* at the New School in New York City. The seminars were recorded on audiotapes, which were donated to the Carnegie Council on Ethics and International Affairs—where Morgenthau had served as a Board member. While the tapes themselves have since been lost, fortunately the seminars were transcribed in 1981, soon after Morgenthau's death. These transcriptions were subsequently compiled and edited by the then president of the Carnegie Council, Dr. Robert J. Myers—himself a former student of Morgenthau—creating a manuscript of approximately 400 pages.

Since that time the manuscript and some related materials have remained at the Carnegie Council. In September 2000 the current council president, Dr. Joel Rosenthal, passed the manuscript on to me to determine whether it would be worth reediting and publishing. Over the next four years I slowly read through them, compared them to Morgenthau's notes and lecture materials from previous classes, discussed them with those more conversant in Morgenthau's work, and reread his published works and the secondary literature about him. The result is the book you hold in your hands.

In this Introduction, I provide some context for this material. I begin by describing Morgenthau's position in the discipline of international relations, explaining why his theories have lost some of their influence in the field. I then suggest a few ways in which these seminars might help reinvigorate an interest in Morgenthau's ideas by orienting the discipline toward some neglected areas of inquiry. I conclude with some explanation of how the seminars were edited by both previous editors and by me.

MORGENTHAU AND THE STUDY OF INTERNATIONAL POLITICS

Hans J. Morgenthau was trained as a lawyer, but claimed he preferred philoso-phy.[1] His decision to study, write on, and teach about international affairs resulted from a feeling of obligation rather than a deep seeded desire.[2] His training in law and appreciation for philosophy is reflected in all of his works, but especially in these seminars on Aristotle. Exploring politics for Morgenthau meant taking on essentially contested concepts, grappling with them, and seeing how they applied to events that are taking place in the world around us. These seminars include his reflections on a host of such concepts, including justice, revolution, equality, free-dom, and law. In deciding how to organize the seminars, I chose to focus on terms such as these, rather than those more commonly associated with Morgenthau, such as the national interest. This not only reflects the subjects of the seminars presented here but also, I believe, Morgenthau's interests in a way that belies his reputation as a theorist of the national interest alone.

But it is as a theorist of the national interest and power politics that Morgenthau is best known in the discipline of international relations. His *Politics among Nations* is generally regarded as his most important contribution to the field, and to-day it remains one of the best-selling textbooks of its kind. Initially considered by some publishers as too idiosyncratic, *Politics among Nations*, published by Alfred A. Knopf in 1948, altered the way in which international relations was taught in the United States. Its mixture of political philosophy, historical case studies, and trenchant analysis makes it accessible to students and scholars alike.

As a result of the success of *Politics among Nations* (it has been through seven editions), Morgenthau's work generated a substantial amount of literature in re-sponse. Some authors argued that Morgenthau was not sufficiently "theoretical" or "scientific" in his theories, such as Kenneth Waltz in *Theory of International Politics*[3] or John Vasquez in *The Power of Power Politics*.[4] Some claimed that Morgenthau and "the realists," as his followers were called, failed to capture trends that challenge the primacy of the nation state, such as the transnationalism of Robert Keohane and Joseph Nye in *Power and Interdependence*.[5] Others chal-

---

1. For historical background on Morgenthau, see "Fragment of an Intellectual Biography: 1904–1932," in *Truth and Tragedy: A Tribute to Hans J. Morgenthau*, 2nd, augmented ed., Kenneth W. Thompson and Robert J. Myers, eds. (New Brunswick, NJ: Transaction Publishers, 1984 [1976]): 1–17; and Christoph Frei, *Hans J. Morgenthau: An Intellectual Biography* (Baton Rouge: Louisiana State University Press, 2001). Morgenthau's papers can be accessed at the Library of Congress, a source upon which Frei drew in writing his biography.

2. See Thompson and Meyers, eds., "Fragment of an Intellectual Biography."

3. Kenneth Waltz, *Theory of International Relations* (Reading, MA: Addison-Wesley Publishers, 1979).

4. John Vasquez, *The Power of Power Politics*, rev. ed. (Cambridge: Cambridge University Press, 1998 [1983]).

5. Robert Keohane and Joseph Nye, *Power and Interdependence: World Politics in Transition* (Boston: Little, Brown, 1977).

lenged Morgenthau on normative grounds, claiming realism left one with little hope for ameliorating conflict, as in Richard Falk's *A Study of Future Worlds*.[6]

These early challenges to Morgenthau evolved into the primary international relations theories of today—neorealism, neoliberalism, postmodernism, and constructivism. While a small group of scholars continues to look to Morgenthau for insights into international relations, the field today is dominated by approaches that derive more from his critics than from Morgenthau himself. Even John Mearsheimer, perhaps the most prominent realist writing today, locates Moregenthau's work in the category of "human nature realism," which he finds defective compared with more recent realist theories.[7] Today, Morgenthau is usually presented as the paradigm "Cold War realist" and as a relic of a "pretheoretical" stage in international relations theory in the discipline of political science.

These early critiques, while perhaps understandable and necessary at the time they were made, misrepresented Morgenthau's ideas. For many, Morgenthau has been reduced to the "six principles of political realism" that were first listed in the second edition of *Politics among Nations*.[8] Those six principles, which were Morgenthau's attempt to respond to some of the criticisms of this work, became enshrined as the most succinct version of realism for students of international relations. Yet they failed to capture the subtlety and depth of his thinking on politics—characteristics that can be found in these seminars and in his numerous other published works.

MORGENTHAU AND THE STUDY OF POLITICS

If Morgenthau's reputation in the discipline of international relations has become solidified as a Cold War realist, can insights from his work be rescued? In these seminars, Morgenthau addresses the work of Aristotle because he saw in the ancient philosopher's method and concerns those akin to his own. Indeed, when asked to list the ten books that meant the most to him, Morgenthau included Aristotle's *The Politics*.[9] In the end, Morgenthau diverges from Aristotle in important ways, but to see how he does this reveals a great deal about how politics can be usefully studied.

These seminars help move us away from a stultified Morgenthau by, first and foremost, revealing a core principle of Morgenthau's thought: Politics is a unique

---

6. Richard Falk, *A Study of Future Worlds* (New York: Free Press, 1975).

7. John Mearsheimer, *The Tragedy of Great Power Politics* (New York: W. W. Norton, 2001), 18.

8. For more information on the sources for and career of *Politics among Nations*, see Kenneth Thompson, "The Writing of Politics among Nations: Its Sources and Its Origins," *International Studies Notes* 24, 1 (1999): 18–22. Thompson, one of Morgenthau's early graduate students, has been the coeditor of all editions of *Politics among Nations*, following the second edition. For the six principles, see Hans J. Morgenthau, *Politics among Nations: The Struggle for Power and Peace*, 6th ed. (New York: Alfred A. Knopf Publishers, 1986), pp. 3–17.

9. Christoph Frei, *Hans J. Morgenthau: An Intellectual Biography*: 113.

realm, one in which certain problems remain perennial. To understand politics, one can look to nuclear weapons policy or the operations of the Mafia in New York City; both cases, which are used throughout these seminars, demonstrate certain truths about politics. This broader understanding of politics is also found in his first published work, *Scientific Man vs. Power Politics*. A book more about epistemology than politics, it sets out a critique of social scientific modes of analysis that continues to ring true to this day.[10] It is also an insight found in *Politics among Nations*, where he writes, "Intellectually, the political realist maintains the autonomy of the political sphere, as the economist, the lawyer, the moralist maintain theirs."[11]

If Morgenthau begins with this core assumption, that the political sphere is unique, are there any insights into his work that might help us to see him differently? More important, are there themes evident in these seminars and his writings more generally that speak to current challenges in the international system? Let me suggest a few potential sources of new insight, sources that derive from these seminars.

First, one of Morgenthau's principal contributions to the study of international relations was the concept of the national interest and its importance in critically evaluating U.S. foreign policy.[12] Taken alone, the national interest does not provide any new insights into how to study international relations, although it is a helpful tool for correcting overly exuberant ideas about the potential for peace through international law and institutions. But when combined with his concept of the national purpose, an idea he articulated in *The Purpose of American Politics* (1965), the two terms together provide an important vantage point from which to think about U.S. foreign policy. The national purpose is the ethos that a country embodies in its principles and actions, in both domestic and foreign policy. Morgenthau stresses that the national interest alone cannot be the sole pursuit of a state's foreign policy:

We know that a real nation worthy of our remembrances has contributed to the affairs of men more than the successful defense and promotion of its national interest. . . . In order to be worthy of our lasting sympathy a nation must pursue its interests for the sake of a transcendent purpose that gives meaning to the day-by-day operations of its foreign policy.[13]

The book focuses on the national purpose of the United States, which he argues rests on two ideas: equality and freedom. These concepts cannot be removed from American foreign policy pursuits, according to Morgenthau, although they must certainly be disciplined by the reality of power politics.

---

10. *Scientific Man vs. Power Politics* (Chicago: University of Chicago Press, 1946).
11. *Politics among Nations*, 6th ed., 13.
12. See his seminal work, *In Defense of the National Interest* (New York: Alfred A. Knopf, 1951), along with his response to critics of that book, "Another Great Debate: The National Interest of the United States," *American Political Science Review* 46, no. 4 (December 1952): 961–988.
13. *The Purpose of American Politics* (New York: Alfred A. Knopf, 1965), 8.

This idea of the national purpose, while not explicitly addressed in these seminars, can be seen throughout them. The basis of Aristotelian political theory is the idea that a polity is not simply designed to provide the space for political interactions among its members, but must also inculcate certain values in its citizens. Morgenthau criticized Aristotle, and his medieval adherents, for contributing to the corporatist, and even fascist, forms of government found in twentieth-century Europe, those forms that assume the state is the wisest and most moral actor. Morgenthau, however, does see in Aristotle's work the importance of moral norms for a successful polity. He debates students, both influenced by his own ideas of the national interest and Marxist thought, who believe that morality has no place in the political realm. Morgenthau's responses sound very much like his idea that there must be a combination of the national purpose and the national interest for a successful polity.

His attempt to combine these concepts comes out most clearly in Chapter 5, "Power, Interests and the Common Good." In these selections, Morgenthau argues that the Aristotelian virtue ethic, especially as manifest in the medieval writings of the scholastics, can lead to injustice and inequality in the political realm. At the same time, he refuses to allow the students to dismiss moral principles, as evidenced in Chapter 4, "Ethics and Politics." Because of his emphasis on power and interests, Morgenthau was accused of failing to take account of law, ethics, and norms in the study of international affairs. Such criticisms fail to see the way in which normative issues are infused throughout his work, including *Politics among Nations*. Morgenthau was intensely interested in the intersection of ethics in politics, themes that emerge in these seminars on Aristotle and are belied by his long association with the Carnegie Council on Ethics and International Affairs.[14]

Does this combination of the national interest and national purpose speak to issues of relevance today? At the time of this writing, the United States is engaged in what the Bush administration calls a "war on terror." This war, conducted on behalf of the entire community of nations, according to the administration, suggests an attempt to combine the national interest with the national purpose. That is, America's war on terrorism is in its own interests but it is also in pursuit of a larger moral purpose for the community of nations.

What would Morgenthau have to say about this war? Would he support it? It is difficult to imagine his response to the attacks of September 11, 2001, and perhaps unfair to try to do so. Rather, the challenge for us is to consider how Morgenthau would analyze the attacks and the U.S. response to them. If one knew only the six principles of realism, along with critiques of them, one might conclude that the American response is understandable as a manifestation of the pursuit of power at the global level. One might also note that the attempt to make a

---

14. Which, to this day, continues to hold an annual Hans J. Morgenthau lecture on ethics and foreign policy; see www.cceia.org for more information on the series and Morgenthau's role as a trustee of the Council.

larger moral campaign out of this war violates the largely relativistic moral structure of the political realm, as stated in principle number 5: "Political realism refuses to identify the moral aspirations of a particular nation with the moral laws that govern the universe."[15]

Do these seminars give us any further insight? The first thing would be that Morgenthau would approach this as a puzzle, something to be investigated according to the structures of political inquiry. His investigation would seek to explore not simply "why" the United States responded as it did to the attacks, but how do we evaluate that response? A possible evaluation can be found in the following passage, where he explores the role of violence in politics:

A system based on force is inherently unstable, like Aristotle's description of a tyrant. Therefore, the need for political conventions and philosophy persist. Certainly with brute force, especially with the kind of force that a modern government possesses, you can do a great deal: you can fill the prisons, you can deport people, you can shoot people. But you cannot really effectively govern them. In order to govern effectively, you have to have the consent of the people. . . . A government is an infinitely complex enterprise. By force you can rise to supreme power, but by force alone you cannot govern. Force remains, as the medieval writers said, the ultimate resort of kings. The term "ultimate" implies that in the day-by-day operations of government, you need certain principles, certain devices, procedures, and institutions. This is what political science or political philosophy deals with.[16]

What does this tell us? Perhaps it tells us that the American response to use force in Afghanistan and Iraq may be an example of "supreme power" but it may not lead to the granting of America the role of legitimate leader of the international system. Although force must play a role in politics, according to politics, when force is divorced from the telos of politics—a concept that Morgenthau explores at great length in chapters 1 and 2 of this volume—you will not be able to effectively govern.

Again, this is not to predict what Morgenthau would say about the American war on terrorism. Rather, it is to draw from his insights suggestions about how the study of this phenomenon might proceed. Only by copying Aristotle's method of combining the empirical with the normative, by orienting the study of politics in accordance with the telos of politics can we be sure that we will arrive at correct and applicable answers.

A second area of Morgenthau's thought that has been neglected also comes from *The Purpose of American Politics*. As noted above, the particular national purpose of the United States, according to Morgenthau, was rooted in the ideas of equality and freedom. These concepts are explored throughout these seminars, where he uses them to examine Aristotle's writings on slavery, women, and revolution. His examination of these ideas through the lens of Aristotle's writing

---

15. *Politics among Nations*, 6th ed., 13.
16. Page 52 in this text.

reveals a scholar who has thought deeply about how these ideas constitute and define the Untied States, especially at a moment when the nation's identity and political purpose was in such flux as it was during the early 1970s.

For Morgenthau, equality and freedom are intimately related. Equality is what differentiates the United States from Europe, especially the Europe that Morgenthau fled because he was Jewish. The importance of equality for Morgenthau prompts him to explore at some depth the status of blacks in the United States, both in these seminars and in some of his published works. He does not, however, simply assert equality as a fact that automatically leads to conformity. Building on Aristotle's notions of equality, he argues that certain forms of functional inequality continue to remain relevant, even in the political sphere. This attempt to rescue from Aristotle some insights on the question of equality is fascinating to observe, especially in his dialogue with students.

Equality leads to an analysis of freedom in these seminars. As he states here, "There is an organic relationship between political power, political equality and political freedom." The relationship results from the fact that to create equality in society you need to limit the freedom of some. This profoundly simple, yet profoundly important, point is one that Morgenthau uses to explore a series of dilemmas in 1970s America. These discussions are particularly revealing, as we see Morgenthau engage an audience of students who were, no doubt, interested in advancing both freedom and equality at a rather turbulent moment in U.S. history.

Does this insight speak to international affairs today? One of the driving questions prompted by the process of economic globalization is the extent to which open borders, free trade, and the movement of capital around the world are improving the freedom and equality of all. Protests against the current international economic system, both from governments and civil society, have raised these issues to a higher degree over the past five years. Can we learn anything from Morgenthau about these global economic issues?

Morgenthau did not write on international economics, nor did he explicitly address questions of economic statecraft. In one published article on foreign aid, he does argue that the provision of aid by great powers should not be seen as a means to improve the economic status of target states, but to improve the great power status of those providing the aid.[17] He also does have a short article on freedom and equality, but its scope of examination is rather limited.[18] When considering his already published works, then, Morgenthau does not provide us much insight into globalization and its consequences for the international system.

These seminars, on the other hand, do reveal some important insights into how we can understand these events. Because he focuses on equality and freedom as core values, and explores them vis-à-vis Aristotle, we can see that he understood the importance of these ideas. Indeed, he notes that equality, freedom, and political

17. "Preface to a Political Theory of Foreign Aid," in Hans J. Morgenthau, *The Restoration of American Politics* (Chicago: University of Chicago Press, 1962), 254–272.
18. "Freedom," in Hans J. Morgenthau, *The Restoration of American Politics*, 71–82.

power are all intertwined in the study of politics, an important corrective to those who assume he saw power as the only issue that defines the political realm. Although he sees these three concepts as linked, he does not give us any easy answers to how to conceptualize their relationship. Rather, he notes that while the ideas of freedom and equality must be the basis of political justice, the practices of politics rarely, if ever, lead to equal and free practices. Calling this an "antinomy" of politics, Morgenthau reveals the complexity of analyzing the political:

And this is the culminating paradox, that a just political order is based upon the principle of equality, but it is in the very nature of politics that it divides men on the basis of inequality. Of course, you can, and in our society we have seen this, you can put the principle of equality above everything else and you are then logically driven toward copping out of politics. . . . My point here is not an anarchist one. . . . I'm fully aware of the inevitability of inequality. I only want to show what the structure of political life is without expressing any preferences or arguing for or against anything.[19]

Again, this does not provide us answers, but it does point us toward directions of inquiry. Rather than seek to find solutions to global economic inequality, Morgenthau is suggesting that we recognize the relationship between a just order in the ideal and the practices that lead to inequality. With this antinomy in mind, we may be able to develop more useful and accurate tools for understanding this global economic dilemma.

A third dimension of Morgenthau's ideas that come forth from these seminars is his interest in and attention to the dilemmas of morality and ethics in the political sphere, especially the role of religion in establishing a normative world order. Greg Russell has argued that Morgenthau synthesized the "normative and empirical halves of theory."[20] In the seminars, as in Morgenthau's published works, there remains some ambiguity about his views on morality. On the one hand, he refuses to accept the students' largely relativist accounts of the political realm, pointing out that our daily discourse is imbued with moral principles. At the same time, he does argue for a larger form of moral relativism, one based on a historical time frame and national context. Reading through his engagement with Aristotle on these questions, especially in chapters 1 and 4, further enhances our understanding of how Morgenthau—and, hence, the discipline of international relations—has sought to balance ethics and politics.

Recent works have tried to locate Morgenthau's ideas of ethics and politics in drastically different intellectual strands. Christoph Frei has sought to pinpoint in Morgenthau's Continental education an interest in and debt to Nietzsche. But, Frei argues, Morgenthau did not go with Nietzsche to the extent of disavowing moral norms. Instead, his position evolved into one that is strikingly similar to Aristotle's:

---

19. Page 61 in this text.
20. See Greg Russell, *Hans J. Morgenthau and the Ethics of American Statecraft* (Baton Rouge: Louisiana State University Press, 1990), 85.

His normative ethics juxtapose the is with the ought to be that is not of this world. They transcend individual existence and reach upward, as it were, toward a heaven of supreme values (hochste Werte) in order to place life under timeless obligations. These values . . . are objective, independent and eternal. The underlying transcendent values, for their part, serve as ultimate goals and also standards for evaluating thought and action.[21]

The idea of values that serve as both goals and standards is strikingly similar to the Aristotelian idea of telos, a concept that Morgenthau addresses at great length in these seminars. Aristotle's combination of empirical investigation and normative purpose clearly matched Morgenthau's method of how to understand the human person and his role in the international political realm.

At the same time, the quote from Frei could also point one toward a religious conception. Benjamin Mollov's recent book on Morgenthau makes this claim, arguing that while he may have disavowed Judaism early in his life (a point Frei makes in examining his diaries), his later life suggests a turn back toward this framework. Along with his aid to Soviet Jews and interest in the state of Israel, Morgenthau's Judaism seemed to influence his ideas of ethics as well. Mollov notes that these seminars (which he read in Morgenthau's papers at the Library of Congress) reveal how Morgenthau saw the importance of the Jewish experience as providing a check on totalitarianism. Mollov also argues that Morgenthau's debt to Reinhold Niebuhr was less as a Christian and more because he provided for Morgenthau an access to the Judeo-Christian scriptures in ways that were relevant for understanding international affairs, especially their prophetic dimension.[22]

The seminars reveal the tension between these two approaches concerning ethics, that is, a naturalist account and a transcendent one. He argues that the Judeo-Christian heritage is an important move away from Aristotle, especially in the creation of transcendent ideals that inform normative ideals from the outside. It is unclear, however, whether or not he sees this move as a positive or negative one. The sections on ethics and politics that I have selected here leave us with a Morgenthau struggling to understand the source of moral norms, but clear that such norms exist and should play a role in the political realm.

Importantly, this tension and ambiguity informs not just Morgenthau's work, but also the role that norms should play in international affairs. American leaders insist on using normative language to define their policies, often putting debates in terms of "good and evil" rather than national interest. But this discourse rarely leads to cooperative policies with either enemies or allies, leaving many to question its utility. Simultaneously, critics of American foreign policy draw on moral principles to argue that the conduct of certain wars and economic policies violate basic norms of peace and justice. Morgenthau himself was impelled to pierce this

---

21. Christoph Frei, *Hans J. Morgenthau: An Intellectual Biography*, 166.
22. See M. Benjamin Mollov, *Power and Transcendence: Hans J. Morgenthau and the Jewish Experience* (Lanham, MD: Lexington Books, 2002), 75–134.

rhetoric and orient the American political community to an honest appraisal of its position in the world. But in so doing, he did not mean to deny that ethics and morality have no role to play in the conduct of foreign policy. His attempt to find a balance between these normative questions informs these seminars as much as it does his writing on foreign policy.

Furthermore, his approach speaks to debates that erupted during the 1990s concerning the ideological orientation of American foreign policy.[23] While Francis Fukuyama proclaimed the "end of history," Samuel Huntington postulated a "clash of civilizations." These debates continued into the late 1990s and early part of the twenty-first century, with Robert Kaplan lamenting the "coming anarchy" and Robert Kagan suggesting that "America is from Mars and Europe is from Venus." These debates are rich with normative implications. Rather than the Cold War policies of containment or deterrence, these new debates cannot assume a single enemy against which the United States should orient its foreign policy. Rather, they suggest that the orientation of the twenty-first century will need to not only find a new enemy but a new normative consensus as well. On top of that, the focus on the Middle East, where religion plays such a strong role in orienting the polities of the region, further complicates the task of finding the right ideological orientation for the United States.

Morgenthau's seminars here suggest an alternative possibility for U.S. foreign policy. Like Aristotle, Morgenthau believed that humanity does contain within him/herself the seeds of moral action. But those seeds cannot be nurtured only in the confines of the sovereign state. Mollov is correct to point to the importance of a transcendent orientation for Morgenthau's ethos, one that comes out clearly in these seminars. When Morgenthau is queried about whether or not "crimes against humanity" are real, he correctly argues that such principles could not exist without the Judeo-Christian tradition providing a pole to orient the human person beyond the sovereign nation-state. Without a religious orientation, ethical norms do not seem sustainable.

This is not to suggest that Morgenthau would advocate making America "a Christian nation," as some neoconservatives would hope. Rather, he is suggesting that one cannot avoid the religious implications of morality. For current debates about American foreign policy, this might suggest that those debates have been lacking an important dimension. Rather than seeing "clashing cultures," we should perhaps find ways to respect and perhaps even agree with some Islamic thinking on international affairs. Scholars who have been working in the interfaith tradition that links Judaism, Christianity, and Islam have argued that there is an "Abrahamic tradition" that can be productively drawn upon to find links with the Islamic world. Rather than trying to convince Islamic countries of the benefits of

---

23. The best collection of the competing ideas can be found in *America and the World: Debating the New Shape of International Politics*, edited by the editors of *Foreign Affairs* (New York: Council on Foreign Relations, 2002).

freedom in terms of material wealth, perhaps it is time to find links between the spiritual heritages of these different faith traditions. Whether or not this is possible without descending into the messianic idealism against which Morgenthau warned should caution us in taking this approach. Nevertheless, it is worth considering as we seek to find answers to how the United States should interact with nations and cultures that seem so alien, yet may perhaps share more of our moral principles than we might at first assume.

These are just a few points that emerge from these seminars, points that reveal the insights Morgenthau has for us today and ones that should help resurrect his reputation in the discipline of international relations. For too long, Morgenthau has been relegated to the category of "Cold War realist." With these seminars, I hope that some of his intellectual acuity and insights on problems old and new will be rekindled.

REGARDING THE TEXT

Editing the spoken record of any scholar requires choices and compromises. The first set of questions concerns where and when the seminars actually took place. The text appears to be a series of graduate level seminars. The dates listed on the transcriptions include fall 1970 and spring 1972. The heading on the manuscript, both those at the Carnegie Council and those in the Library of Congress, state that these seminars were conducted at the New School of Social Research in New York City. The first page of the manuscript lists the course as Political Science U719, with a beginning date of September 18, 1970, a Friday. The dates through 1970 continue to be on Fridays, going through mid-December, which would correspond to an academic semester. The courses listing 1971 and 1972 have dates in the spring, roughly late January through May. In contacting some of Morgenthau's students, I also discovered that he had taught a course on Aristotle every year from 1956 to 1966 at the University of Chicago.[24]

Further investigation into the source of the manuscript, however, raised some problems. To begin with, according to Christoph Frei, Morgenthau was a visiting professor at the New School from 1971 to 1974. This would make a lecture starting in the fall of 1970 at the New School unlikely.[25] Via correspondence with the archivist at the New School, I discovered that Morgenthau is not listed as teaching any course in the political science department during the year 1970, nor were courses designated by the letter U. Further, the course catalogue lists a course taught by Professor Howard White on Aristotle's *The Politics*, but it was not offered in the fall 1970 semester.

Two possibilities suggest themselves. First, Morgenthau was also a visiting professor at the City College of New York during this time, from 1969 to 1971. It

---

24. Personal e-mail contact from Professor Kenneth Thompson, University of Virginia, March 8, 2004.
25. Christoph Frei, *Hans Morgenthau: An Intellectual Biography*, 75, fn. 51.

may be that he offered the seminars at the City College rather than the New School. Another possibility is that the date of 1970 was incorrectly listed on the manuscript. The lectures could have been given over the course of a single year at the New School, probably 1971–1972. This, however, would still not explain his absence from the New School's course catalogues.

Robert Myers, who undertook to have the seminars published in 1983, stated in a letter to an editor at W. W. Norton the following explanation for the source of the text:

Some time in the early 1970s, Hans gave me some of the tapes of this lecture series which was [sic] done at the New School for Social Research in 1970, 1971, and 1972. A word on a number of them, particularly those of September 1970. As you know, I encouraged Hans to try to develop a book from that series which resulted in the contract with either Liveright or Norton. He never quite got around to working on the manuscript, for reasons of health, and for that reason I was given the material by his two children.[26]

Certain references in the text also suggest that the lectures were given at least up through 1972; for example, he cites Nixon's visit to China, which took place in February 1972. Consequently, I can only conclude with certainty that the seminars were conducted at a university in the New York City area during the period 1970–1972. Precisely which university and which course remain uncertain.

The seminars have been edited twice, once by Robert Myers and a second time by me.[27] The first time, Myers had the seminars transcribed, transcriptions that he then read through and edited. In some cases he took out student questions and clarified certain phrases. Because the actual audiotapes no longer seem to exist, I cannot compare Myers' editing with the original material. Myers, however, was both a student of Morgenthau's and a friend. The fact that Morgenthau gave the tapes to Myers to transcribe and perhaps publish suggests that his editing reflected, in part, Morgenthau's original wishes.

Myers' editing took the student questions out of about half the material. In my editing, I removed some other students' questions, but left in those that remained essential to understanding the progress of the text. In other words, where a student's questions could be elided with a simple, "Consider the question of . . .", I removed it. If it took Morgenthau in an entirely different direction, I kept it in. This makes the text less fluid at times, but it does, as a result, accurately reflect the way in which his thinking developed.

I think it is also useful to retain some of the questions from students in as much as they illuminate Morgenthau's engagement with the intellectual currents of his day. The students' concerns with Marxism, race, and Vietnam all reflect issues that must have informed Morgenthau's thinking on these matters. His reactions to

---

26. Letter of Robert J. Myers to Mr. Victor Schmalzer, W. W. Norton and Co., June 1, 1983.
27. They have also been copyedited by John Tessitore and Liz Leiba, some of whose insights were more substantive than simply grammatical, for which I am very appreciative.

certain questions also reveal his attitudes toward certain trends in American intellectual life at the time. These revelations further inform our understanding of Morgenthau's position on various debates during this era.

I have also taken the liberty of moving certain sections of the text in order to create six chapters that address six distinct themes. As a result, the seminars no longer reflect a historical progression, a change that emphasizes the ideas rather than their actual presentation. Because the seminars were given over the course of three years, I have also deleted certain repetitive sections, that is, examples he uses more than once and entire sections that appear to be copied from earlier seminars.

Finally, I have added a number of footnotes to explain many of Morgenthau's more obscure or lesser-known contextual references. These references also reflect a wide range of scholarly books and debates in which he must have been interested. For example, he twice mentions debates about the meaning of the French Revolution, citing rather obscure historians as evidence of different interpretations. These references were rather difficult to find, both because the transcriber occasionally wrote the name incorrectly, and because some are from nineteenth century books that are no longer readily available.

The translation of Aristotle that Morgenthau used is most likely that of Benjamin Jowett, which is reproduced in Richard McKeon's collection of Aristotle's works.[28] At certain points, Morgenthau quotes Aristotle directly, and those quotes are verbatim representations of Jowett's translation. Morgenthau's interpretation of Aristotle is rather standard, following most of the currents in philosophical analyses of Aristotle. Aristotle was not new to Morgenthau. We have a copy of lecture notes, typed by a student, on *The Politics* from 1948 in Morgenthau's papers at the Library of Congress. As I point out in the footnotes to one section, Morgenthau's interpretation of certain passages in Aristotle in these seminars does not differ much from his 1948 seminars.

In closing, I acknowledge that some readers might be concerned that because of the two editing stages, the loss of the original tapes, and the confusion about when and where these seminars were conducted, that they do not accurately reflect Morgenthau's ideas. I struggled with this concern myself at various times in the editing of these seminars. But in preparing to edit them, I came across the following discussion of the writings of Aristotle, whose writings were undoubtedly edited by his students. One student in particular, Andronicus, probably did the final editing. Jonathan Barnes has this to say about the editing and reading of Aristotle:

Andronicus will hardly have modified the content of Aristotle's views; and it is plain that he did not tamper much with the style. But no doubt he did a small amount of editorial work: he probably added some cross-references, and he may have interpolated an occasional sentence to link one essay in a treatise to its successor. . . . It is difficult to read a text

---

28. Richard McKeon, ed., *The Basic Works of Aristotle* (New York: Random House, 1941), 1127–1325.

in this way. It is also challenging—and fun. There are dangers: disciplined reading softens into imaginative interpretation—and then into free association. But the dangers can be avoided. And there is really no other way to take these texts.[29]

Indeed, there is no other way to take Morgenthau's texts; they should be read as they were edited, true to Morgenthau's ideas but leading to "imaginative interpretation."

---

29. Jonathan Barnes, "Life and Work," in *The Cambridge Companion to Aristotle*, edited by Jonathan Barnes (Cambridge: Cambridge University Press, 1995), 14–15.

CHAPTER 1

Politics and Political Science

Our discussion is going to correlate the political thought of Aristotle with contemporary political problems. It appears at first sight to be a somewhat remote and academic enterprise. Naturally you will ask yourself what has an old guy who lived almost 2500 years ago to tell us about contemporary political problems. If you were to deal with contemporary technical or scientific problems, you wouldn't dream of going back to the Greeks and trying to learn from them the answers to our problems. However, there are two fundamental facts that make any political philosopher, and more particularly, a political philosopher of the greatness of Aristotle, relevant to our time. For as you will see when you take even a superficial look at Aristotle's *The Politics*—or a superficial look at the history of any political community—in contrast to the technical and scientific problems, social and political problems do not change through history. The problem of authority, the problems of the relations between the individual and the state, the purpose of the state, the common good, the issue of law versus naked power, the problem of violence, the class problem, the distribution of wealth in political terms—all those problems are of a perennial nature. They have not been discovered or invented in the twentieth century. You can read any political writer—the prophets of the Old Testament or Indian political philosophers, not to speak of Confucius and the ancient Greeks—and you will find that they deal with essentially the same problems which baffle us today, and upon the understanding and solution of which our own welfare and our own orderly and just political society depends.

Thus, the first justification of trying to correlate Aristotle's political thought with our contemporary political problems lies in the fact of the immutability of

---

This section includes seminars from September 18 and September 26, 1970.

our political problems. The other justification lies in the nature of Aristotle's political thought. When you read Aristotle for the first time, it appears to you that this is plain common sense. It's very simple, and there's really very little to it. You read it the next time and you discover things you never thought of before and had never seen in Aristotle before. Every time you read him, you find something new, something relevant, profound in a seemingly simple and almost commonsensical formulation. The more often you read Aristotle, your experience will bear out what I have said. In other words, the experience one has with Aristotle is not dissimilar to the experience one has with Greek art, more particularly Greek sculpture. You look at a Greek sculpture and you find it beautiful and of classic simplicity, but the more often you look at it you discover new meanings, new suggestions that escaped you the first time. The relevance of Aristotle to our political problems lies in both the perennial character of our political problems and the enormous profundity of Aristotle's political thought.

While his political thought, as all great political thought, received its stimulation from contemporary political problems and tried to respond to those contemporary political problems, he transcended those problems by formulating what one might call eternal verities about the nature of politics and the nature of man. What I have just said, you might be thinking to yourself, is not the prevailing academic opinion. A great number of political scientists—the great majority of political scientists—would regard an enterprise like this an old-fashioned undertaking that cannot possibly have any meaning for modern political science, modern political philosophy, and for the practical solution and philosophic understanding of contemporary political problems. Any behaviorist, anyone who believes that quantification is tantamount to truth and that the number of charts and equations you put into your paper or book is indicative of your objectivity and the profundity of your thought will scoff at this kind of thing.

On a higher level of philosophic sophistication you have an argument that the prevailing modern school of philosophy—logical positivism—makes not only against Aristotle as a political thinker but also against traditional philosophy as such. The argument runs approximately, in an oversimplified form, as follows: Traditional philosophy deals with apparent problems, what is called in German *Scheineproblem*, problems which are not real but are the result of a false formulation of the problem. It is the purpose of philosophy, the real legitimate purpose of philosophy, to show the false character of the problems as formulated by traditional political philosophy, to clarify the meaning of the concepts that traditional philosophy uses. The discovery of the "meaning of meaning" is one of the main, if not *the* main, purposes of this predominant philosophic school, so that logical positivism really becomes a kind of semantics, a kind of reducing of traditional philosophic concepts to their core meaning, and thereby showing how useless, misguided this traditional political philosophy is. The most influential, and also the most consistent manifestation of this school of thought in political philosophy is Karl Popper, author of *The Open Society and*

Its Enemies.[1] Popper subjects all major political philosophers to this kind of positivistic logical analysis and arrives at a foregone conclusion: No traditional political philosopher has thought straight, that they all have been terribly mixed up and they ought to be discarded, and the only thing that is left is this common sense and new excursion into the higher reaches of political philosophy.

Aristotle cannot be understood without reference to Plato, of whom he was a disciple and whose philosophy he both developed and contradicted. Neither Plato nor Aristotle can be understood without reference to the Sophists, the school of philosophy that both Plato and Aristotle tried to demolish through argument and which was the dominant school of philosophy in Greece. We now identify Plato and Aristotle as the main representatives of Greek philosophy. But, historically speaking, they were outsiders. They didn't belong to the philosophic establishment. They were nonconformists. They wouldn't have been elected president of the Greek political association, and they wouldn't have been invited to the Athenian White House nor would their pieces have been printed in the Greek political science review, if there were such a thing. In other words, they were the nonorthodox dissenters.

The Sophists were the orthodox, respectable representatives of philosophy and, more particularly, political philosophy. The negative, pejorative connotation that attaches today to the term Sophist and Sophism was completely absent in contemporary Greece. It is a result of the very effective job of demolition that Plato and Aristotle have done. We have to distinguish between our evaluative perspective concerning Plato and Aristotle on the one hand and the Sophists on the other in the contemporary perspective of Athens. The Sophists were the respectable ones, the ones to whom the better classes of Athens sent their children to be educated. Socrates was the seducer of the youth, the man who alienated the Athenian youth from the orthodox truth. If you want to go to extremes, you could say that Socrates was like Paul Goodman in our period, or men like Fiedler, who stand at the margin of society intellectually and socially and are experienced as a threat, with good reason, to society.[2]

After all, Socrates didn't die as an honored member of the establishment. He was executed. He was executed not because of a whim of the Athenian powers that be, but because intellectually he was a threat to the intellectual status quo, to the establishment, to the powers that be. One has to keep this in mind when one tries to assess the political function those philosophers performed for Athenian intellectual life and Athenian society. The intellectual superiority over the

---

1. Karl Popper, *The Open Society and Its Enemies*, rev. ed. (Princeton: Princeton University Press, 1950).
2. Paul Goodman (1911–1972) was a social critic and writer who lived in New York City, whose book, *Growing Up Absurd*, made him a hero to the antiestablishment movements of the 1960s. I believe Morgenthau is also referring to Leslie Fiedler (1920–2003), a literary critic who was known for his iconoclastic style and ideas.

philosophers of the establishment gave them the aura of greatness and orthodoxy that we now attach to them. But in their own time they were the outsiders, the dangerous men, the people who had to be kept at arm's length, or even to execute in order to protect the intellectual and political status quo.

This transformation of the political function that thinkers perform is a general one. You have only to look at Christianity. The early Christians—Christ, the Apostles—were also revolutionaries. After all, Christ was executed not for his religious beliefs but because of his political subversion. He claimed to be the King of the Jews. There was another king who was in power and there were political institutions which were not willing to countenance a subversive revolutionary claim to the throne of Israel. So Christ was executed. The early Christians who had to hide in the catacombs and who were executed as enemies of the state were not primarily executed for their religious beliefs, but for the political implications of their religious beliefs. Their religious beliefs stipulated that there was a power beyond and above the Roman Emperor; that the Roman Emperor was not a godhead and the ultimate source of absolute political truth, but that there was a source of truth and power to which the Roman Emperor was subject. And this the Roman powers that be could not accept.

You have a very similar situation today in the relations between totalitarian powers and certain groups within the societies. For example, the position of the Jews in the Soviet Union has its ultimate source in exactly this historic relationship between the early Christians and the Roman Empire. This is true not only of the Soviet Jews, but also to a greater or lesser extent of Jewish communities everywhere.[3] It is not possible for them to admit that a political power is the ultimate source of political truth. That is, no religion of a transcendental nature can admit that a secular, political system is not subject to some higher power and that its political truth does not have to be judged by the truth emanating from that higher power. Such a position is obviously unacceptable to any totalitarian political power or to any political power that claims a monopoly of truth.

Individuals who are faced by this claim of the state often accept it, voluntarily or not. Others resist in the name of other moral standards. What we call conscience as the source of these moral judgments has to have a point of reference that goes beyond the individual. Here you have the state, which claims a monopoly on all values—political, moral, and otherwise. Here you have the individual who has a conscience and who opposes the state or at least submits the state to judgments that do not emanate from the state itself. Where do they emanate from? The individual opposing the state, taking his life in his hands, cannot rely upon that vague opposition to the state. He has to find a point of reference from which his conscience gets the assurance that what he considers to be the true moral

3. Morgenthau was actively engaged in attempts to aid and free Soviet Jewry, especially through his work with the American Committee for Soviet Jewry. See M. Benjamin Mollov, *Power and Transcendence: Hans J. Morgenthau and the Jewish Experience* (Lanham, MD: Lexington Books, 2002), 135–172.

values are really moral values. This you can only find from a source that is above the state. If you look at the opposition to Nazism from within Germany, most of the opponents either found the assurance that they were on the right track from religion or from Marxism, which is also a religion.

Not every political philosophy, however, is a religion because some philosophies are relativistic, and not sure of having the truth. Look at the confrontation between Christ and Pontius Pilate. It is the classic example of one absolutist who has the truth: "I am the King of the Jews" or "I am the Son of God," and Pontius Pilate who asks: "What is truth?" He submits the claim to absolute truth to a democratic referendum. The majority decides. He asks the crowd: "Whom do you want? Jesus of Nazareth or Barabbas?"[4] And you know what the vote was. It has not been confirmed by history.

The individual—and you can test this by your own experience—is not self-confident enough to take the risk of standing up and saying, "The state is wrong and I say so at the risk of my being crushed by the State." He needs to have an objective point of reference that assures him that his opposition to the state is not just a quixotic whim, but also the expression of an objective truth. Where does he find that assurance? He finds it either in otherworldly or in a secular religion. And it works the other way around. The opposition of the Nazis to the republic (even though the risks were remote) was also based upon a firm though not very serious conviction that Hitler was the Messiah who had been sent by the Teutonic god to the German people to redeem them, to save them, and that his word was the truth.

The secular revolutionary who says, "I have been suppressed. I have been exploited by this society. This society from which I come is unjust and I'm going to change it or destroy it," certainly is opposed to the status quo, to the state, to the powers that be. But not in the name of a higher law, a higher principle, but simply on the basis of, you may say, his ethnic or class or whatever interests. He says, "I don't have my share. And I want it. And I shall get it. And either I shall get it by radical reform or, if that doesn't work, I will get it by revolution." But this is something quite different. This is an old dispute, an old controversy that was created by the French Revolution.

The French historians of the French Revolution raised the question, "What is responsible for the Revolution? On behalf of what was that revolution made?" One school of thought under the leadership of Professor Aulard said, "The ideas of the French Revolution, Rousseau and of course, the Enlightenment, the encyclopedists—they created the French Revolution." Others said, "They made the Revolution because they did not want to starve to death."[5]

---

4. This version of the confrontation between Jesus and Pilate is found in only one of the four Christian Gospels, John 18:28–40.

5. Alphonse Aulard (1849–1928) was a professor at the University of Paris and is considered one of the first "professional" historians of the French Revolution. I was not able to access his works directly, so I am unclear as to the details of the controversy to which Morgenthau refers here.

Now generally and typically, this physical intolerability of the status quo requires an ideological justification. They are not going to go into the street and
risk death simply because they have not enough earthly goods. They are going
to make a revolution stimulated by this lack of earthly goods because they believe in a truth that the powers that be have corrupted or neglected and that they
are going to help to triumph over the forces of darkness. It is exactly because
you speak and act on behalf of such a truth that you have the confidence that in
the end the truth will win out, that virtue will prevail over evil, and that you are
the instrument of the powers which, even if you were not acting, would still prevail. This gives the revolutionary the courage to go into the streets and risk his
life.

Consider another example: the Bolshevist Revolution of 1917. It certainly would
not have succeeded if the peasants didn't want peace. In this war, the basic issue
would be the provisional government of Kerensky against Lenin. Kerensky wanted
to continue [World War I] and Lenin said, "No, we want peace." So, in this contest
between two objectives, the desire of the peasants for peace and of the general
population of an end to the war won out. But as soon as the civil war started, you
had to have on the part of the revolutionary some kind of faith, some kind of belief in a truth for which they were fighting that was superior to the truth, the appearance of truth, for which the other side was fighting. And here Bolshevism
came in. Marxism, Leninism came in. Because when you read the pieces that
Lenin wrote during the Revolution and the civil war, this becomes perfectly clear.
The very fact that a revolutionary leader like Lenin felt the compulsion to go into
his study from a street fight or from directing the revolution and write a piece
about infantile leftism ("What is to be done"), imperialism, or the last phase of
capitalism, shows the absolute necessity for a revolutionary movement to have a
doctrine, to feel itself in the possession of a truth which will lead it to victory.[6]
Lenin did not have a received truth, you may say; he had to manufacture, to create
the truth while he went along with the revolution.[7]

When we speak of Sophists, we attach a negative, a pejorative judgment to the
term. But you can see even from the etymology of the term that it originally had
a positive connotation. Because what does Sophism mean? The term sophism
comes from *sophia*, which is wisdom. Those were the men of wisdom, the

---

6. Morgenthau refers to various writings by Lenin, including the famous essay, "*What Is to Be Done*,"
his work on imperialism, and some of his polemics against opponents in the early period of the Bolshevik movement. See Robert C. Tucker, ed., *The Lenin Anthology* (New York: W. W. Norton and
Company, 1975).

7. Morgenthau is referring here to the events that took place in Russia between February 1917 and
October 1917, when the Provisional Government, led by Alexander Kerensky, took control of Russia from the monarchy. One of the most important issues facing Russia during this period was
whether or not they should continue to fight in what was known as the Great War (later known as the
First World War). The Provisional Government authorized a major offensive during this period,
which many believe contributed to its downfall as such a strategy rapidly lost it allies among the
workers.

philosophers. And the intellectual demolition by Plato and Aristotle of the Sophist position was a direct attack against the social structure that the Sophists ideologically justified and rationalized. The position of the Sophists was very simple. It was completely relativistic. You have in Plato's *Republic* the famous dialogue between Socrates and Thrasymachus about the nature of justice. And Thrasymachus says that justice is the right of the stronger.[8] And so you have what you call today a power political interpretation and also a relativistic interpretation of political philosophy in which there is really no objective criterion for judging a political event one way or the other. Whoever is at the top is right because he happens to be at the top.

There is no transcendent judgment or criterion available that would make an objective judgment possible. If you look in contemporary political science and you see, for instance, the pressure-group theory or any behaviorist and so-called empirical political science, it is exactly the same thing. It accepts whatever power relations exist as a given. They may explain it, elaborate it, try to improve it, try to change it, at least within narrow limits, but to render judgment on objective philosophic grounds with regard to a particular distribution of power would be regarded as an illegitimate enterprise, as subjective, as the introduction of subjective values into what is called a value-free political science; in other words as an illegitimate, scientifically irrelevant enterprise. There is no such thing as a value-free political science. There is not even such a thing as a value-free medicine. Medicine, obviously, has a conception of the normal functioning of the body. It also has a conception of health, which determines its activities, which gives its activities a teleological point of reference. Indeed, the purpose of medicine is to protect health by preventing disease or, if disease occurs, to restore the body to health.

When you take a look at politics, a value-free political science is of course by definition a status quo, a conservative, a conformist political science because it accepts the prevailing values of political society as a datum of nature, which political science analyzes, reforms, embroiders, justifies, and rationalizes. But the idea that you can escape valuation implicit or explicit in politics is a result not only of a fundamental misunderstanding of the nature of politics but also of a conformist, conservative position for which positivism, objectivity, relativity become ideological weapons with which they defend their own position as an intellectual enterprise as well as the existing distribution of political power.

It is, of course, possible to have a political science that embraces certain values explicitly and that is also conservative. Take, for instance, the political philosophy of absolute monarchy: that is, the legitimation of monarchy, in terms of the grace of God, so that the monarch governs by the grace of God and he is the exponent of the will of God as long as he obeys the divine command. But in our period of intellectual history, this kind of open justification of a particular power situation in

---

8. See Plato, *The Republic*, Book 1, sections 338b–339a for Thrasymachus' famous challenge to Socrates.

terms of theological arguments is, of course, no longer acceptable because other-worldly religion itself has lost its plausibility for the great mass of intellectuals and peoples at large. So you have to substitute for the open, clear-cut, unabashed reference to some supreme value that justifies the status quo. You have to substitute for that implicit ideology that is provided by positivism, by accepting the status quo as a given that is not to be questioned, at least not be questioned in legitimate philosophic or scientific terms.

Sophism is not a phenomenon that is limited to ancient Greece and it is not in its historic context a disreputable phenomenon. You may say it is a perennial, intellectual, and social configuration. Our Sophists, in objective terms, are a prevailing political science performing the same intellectual and political function for our society that the ancient Sophists performed for the society of Athens. I would not know who are the Aristotles and Platos of our period of history; we have to wait for history to decide that. There may be none. What is interesting is the great difference between our intellectual situation and the situation of ancient Greece. The Greeks had confidence in the ability of reason, of secular reason, to find the truth and to prove the truth, this is to say, to separate truth from error in a convincing, objective way.

In ancient Greece the religious myths lost their plausibility, as our religious myth has lost its plausibility. Philosophy took over and had the confidence to find a secular truth that was as true as any mythological truth and certainly superior to the relativistic position of the Sophists simply by the innate powers of reason. You may say that the flowering of the great idealistic philosophic systems in Western civilization, Hegel, Schelling,[9] were the equivalent of this Platonic and Aristotelian confidence in the powers of reason to find the objective truth and to demonstrate its validity. Something happened in our society in the nineteenth century that happened also in Greece but was very quickly suppressed by neo-Platonism, and that is the rise of empirical science.

Empirical science, experimental science, devalued not only otherworldly religion but also secular philosophy because it became obvious that there was a different and more plausible truth in the discoveries of science than in the philosophic speculations of Hegel. And so, science has destroyed not only our faith in otherworldly religion but also our faith in the power of reason to discover the truth and to demonstrate its validity. The impasse in which we find ourselves today, philosophically speaking, is the result of this destructive attack of science upon philosophy—the result of the demonstration by science that there is a truth beyond which science can discover and make plausible and which philosophy cannot.

So it is not by accident that Marx, trying to develop a new political philosophy that would at the same time be a guide to action, did not undertake to replace, let

---

9. Georg W. F. Hegel (1770–1831) and Friedrich Wilhelm Joseph Schelling (1775–1854), two of the most important representatives of the German School of philosophical "idealism."

me say, the philosophic system of Hegel with another one, but to develop a science of society, the one in opposition to Hegel.

As Marx put it, "Hegel has put the philosophy on its head; I shall put it back on its feet." And so the purpose of Marx was to create an empirical social science similar to the natural sciences that would discover and demonstrate the same kind of inescapable, ineluctable truth that the natural sciences were discovering every day. It is a very open question whether he succeeded, but in any case, this was his purpose. So, the purpose was really anti-philosophical. And the great intellectual function and achievement of Marx was the attempt to create or to substitute for the discredited metaphysical systems an objective social science that in its empirical objectivity and plausibility would be the equal of the natural sciences.

Where did Plato and Aristotle find the source of objective truth? How did they prove or try to prove that there was an objective truth? How do you prove there was an objective concept of justice? And that justice was not as thought, simply the right of the stronger? Justice was simply what the stronger would say it was. How did they prove it? Plato proved it by referring to the ideas, the objective truth that lay behind the shadows of our sensual perception. What we see is not the truth. The truth is the idea of the chair, or the rational conception of a chair. And so, in the famous allegory of the cave, what we see is the shadows on the wall made by the sun. But the essence of the truth is understood to be what the shadow on the wall of the cave actually did represent. It is called in German the *Urbild*, the fundamental, and the primordial concept of what we see with our senses. Here is a chair. What is behind that chair, what is the idea of the chair? I can't go into detail and I'm not going to provide you with a critical analysis of this conception. But this was the conception of the source of the truth in Plato.

The Aristotelian conception of the truth was something quite different, something much more empirical. It was the telos, that is to say, purpose, the ultimate aim toward which an empirical phenomenon aspired. Take the phenomenon of the acorn. Here is an empirical object. It has an innate telos, an innate purpose to become an oak tree. And the oak tree is pre-figured in the acorn. This is an empirical fact. And so, according to Aristotle, all empirical phenomena have an innate teleological purpose, an innate teleological drive toward becoming what, according to nature, they are supposed to become. So the state, the political society has a teleological purpose, an innate purpose that one has to discover by reason. Then one can establish a rational political system that is best fitted to achieve that purpose. But it has that purpose even without such philosophic enlightenment. It has it because it exists.

Science has to have certain cognitive principles. We approach reality with an implicit and inchoate set of values that we want to discover. Empirical reality is infinitely varied and quantitatively not subject to assimilation. So whatever empirical study we make by way of selection from an enormous number of empirical data, the principle of selection is a value. For instance, I could make it my purpose of empirical investigation to count the number of hairs on your head, which, in terms of value, is not a particularly revealing or interesting activity. So, by studying one thing and leaving aside a hundred others, you already apply a value. We are philosophers without knowing it.

It is impossible to have an empirical method that is the end-all and be-all of social investigation. Any social investigation, if it is not utterly mechanical like counting the number of cobblestones or measuring their size, receives its sense and meaning from a philosophic presupposition. That presupposition may be unconscious, inchoate, or unsophisticated. But it exists. Why are we here discussing Aristotle in relation to contemporary political problems? Because we assume philosophically, without having any proof of this at the moment, and without having any sophistication about it, that the study of contemporary political problems makes sense, has a meaning, and that the thought of Aristotle makes sense with regard to those contemporary problems and has a meaning for them.

There is an enormous amount of empirical investigation in sociology, in economics, in political science that is completely meaningless because it has no relation to what anybody would like to know and what is worth knowing. I remember a study that I read long ago in a journal of sociology. It was a study made in a Massachusetts hospital about particular sexual practices—just for the heck of it, just statistics, so often in this street and so often in another street, Catholics so often, Protestants so often. . . . You ask yourself what for? There appears to be absolutely no point to it.

For instance, in California an enormous study with enormous expenditures has been made about the social background of county judges. I happen to be on friendly terms with one of the researchers (you see philosophic positions do not necessarily lead to personal animosity; they sometimes do, however) and I asked my friend, "What's the point of all this?" The fellow looked at me and said, "That question has never occurred to me." Here was something we don't know yet. Why don't we try to find out? You might count the leaves on trees and it would make exactly as much sense. And if the counting of leaves were a social or political phenomenon, we would have done it long ago and [some] foundation would have given us half a million dollars. I'm not joking.

The avoidance of values, the engaging in meaningless empirical investigation has, of course, also a positive political effect. Because it makes it appear that we live, politically speaking, in the best of all possible worlds. There aren't any real political problems. That this is all we need to do and otherwise everything is in good shape. Take any of the real political problems we are facing and you will find that political science has not recognized that they exist. For instance, look at what I have called the new feudalism, that is to say, the political power of private government, corporations, and labor unions, which is as important a political phenomenon in our society as was the power of the feudal lords in the Middle Ages. Nobody has ever even mentioned this phenomenon. It doesn't exist. Because if you recognize it, you become controversial. And nothing can be worse for your academic career, for your standing, your reputation in the profession than being controversial. But being not controversial in the political realm is to be irrelevant.

Take the issue of minorities, the political position of blacks, the political position of the underclass in our society. Who has dealt with them in political science? Neither black nor white political scientists have until very recently recognized the existence of those problems.

Consider the political system of the Mafia, which is a state, a political organization with an executive, legislative, and judicial branch, which has principles of morality, which has laws that are obeyed and if they are not obeyed, enforced, which is a political organization, and which has direct relevance to, you may say, a subterranean or an illegitimate political organization, which has direct relevance for the legitimate political organization because it interacts with it. The Mafia is a very important factor in the way our political system operates because it influences elections and the activities of judges, legislators, and the police. I remember one colleague in Chicago who had very good personal relations with the Mafia and talked to them and investigated certain aspects of their activities, but even if they are not obviously fully open to investigation, you can at least state the problem, that there is an issue and what the intellectual possibilities are, the theoretical possibilities, and we have a great deal of data.

The Mafia is all around us. I used to go occasionally to the barbershop in the Waldorf Astoria Hotel at 11:00 just to watch the operations of Mr. Costello who got a shave there every day.[10] (If you want to make a case of it, why don't you have a shave yourself, or have your hair cut. Some of you are ready for that.) I was fascinated. He held court. There were a number of figures around which you could identify from their appearance up to a certain point as to their function. There was one guy who was obviously the Lord Executioner of the outfit. I mean, that's the way he looked. And somebody would come and would give him a little slip of paper with a figure on it. He would look at it, cut it into the smallest possible pieces and throw it into a kind of a spittoon, or whatever it was. I don't think the Waldorf Astoria has spittoons, but it was some kind of container. And there was a very elegant fellow who was obviously a procurer who whispered to the manicure girls and made dates for them. You could see from the embarrassed faces of the girls that this was obviously what it was. And so you have a whole society here. If one would investigate, if one would analyze what was said and look at the court record and would interview police officials, FBI people and politicians, one could learn a great deal. One wouldn't learn exactly how much money was spent or changed hands, which is not necessary; but the mechanics of one political organization and, more particularly, the interaction with another political organization is a fascinating thing. It is subject to investigation. You see, even if you look at legitimate political processes, the possibility of empirical investigation is limited because you cannot get at the papers of contemporary political figures or even those who are close to being contemporary political figures. The witnesses will not tell you everything or

---

10. I believe Morgenthau is referring to Frank Costello, a major Mafia figure in New York during the mid-twentieth century.

they will tell you the story that they want you to hear. In other words, you have to use your own judgment that this is the way history is written. And political analysis is vague. But the point I am making is that there is a whole field of political phenomena that is taboo, which for the official political science does not exist.

The understanding of a political problem requires answers to a series of questions: What are the forces that mold this political problem? What are the potentialities of those political forces? What is the distribution of power? How is it controlled? How does it change? Those are all empirical, analytical tasks from which certain practical tasks in regard to reform may follow, but not necessarily so. But those analytical tasks are not performed. Now you have a point when you ask, "How do I know that my analysis reveals a truth that a strictly behavioral analysis does not reveal?" Now I have no guaranty that what I say is true, but at least I deal with problems that obviously, on the basis of rational investigation, are important, are relevant. The relationship between economic forces and the legislature or the administrative agencies is, I think, an important problem. On this we can all agree because we all have a rational faculty to understand the significance of political problems.

It is interesting, for instance, that a single individual like Mr. Nader[11] has done more to illuminate those problems than political scientists. Or that a theologian like Reinhold Niebuhr has made the greatest contemporary contribution to the understanding of basic political problems and not a professor of political theory.[12] Reason tells us that certain problems are important and the application of reason to the analysis of those problems in greater detail is subject to empirical investigation. I can make the philosophic statement that the balance of power is the crux of international relations, which is a rational statement posing a particular political problem. But then this statement, which is in a sense an *a priori* philosophic statement, guides my empirical investigation, gives meaning to my empirical investigation because I can then look at their actions and see that throughout history people have thought and statesmen have thought and have tried to act in terms of the balance of power. But if I didn't have this cognitive hypothesis, I wouldn't have been able to develop a theory on international relations. So you have an a priori principle that is based, of course, on empirical investigation. The empirical investigation will prove to what extent your hypothesis was correct or incorrect. But if you start by investigating the number of children county judges in California have, you are already lost in a maze of irrelevant empirical facts because you haven't got a philosophic hypothesis.

The persistence of the pattern of the balance of power shows me that the theory in practice of the balance of power is not the result of the whims of statesmen or of an ephemeral historic situation but of the nature of things because wherever

11. Ralph Nader, political activist, 1934– .
12. Reinhold Niebuhr, Christian pastor and theologian (1871–1972), whom Morgenthau called "the father of us all," referring to the influence Niebuhr had on the realists.

you look, wherever there exists a multiplicity of autonomous social units that want to preserve their autonomy, we have the pattern of the balance of power. You have it in the family, in the mother-in-law situation; the typical conflict situation is a balance of power situation, status quo policy on the one hand and imperialism on the other. And so on, on all levels of social interaction. This is what the original hypothesis helps you understand.

The concept of the balance of power leads you to a caution with regard to proposals for radical change. The principles people have followed since time immemorial have, of course, certain plausibility because they have been followed. There is no argument in favor of their being sound *a priori*, yet it stands to reason that if you and I are autonomous, we have no superior above us, we live in social conflict. You have the intention to subvert my autonomy and I have the intention to subvert yours. There are only two ways in which we can protect our autonomy: one, by the balance of power, where I have sufficient power to protect myself and you know it, and you have sufficient power to protect yourself and I know it. Two, we have a superior who is strong enough to restrain both of us from infringing upon our autonomy, which means, of course, a loss of our respective autonomy to a superior. This is the Hobbesian solution. This is the solution of world government. But it all follows from certain basic philosophic assumptions about the balance of power.

We are trying to find an objective basis for the understanding not only of politics, but also of man and the universe.[13] I explored how both Plato and Aristotle tried to find an objective distinction between opinion and truth, which lies in the obsolescence of the theological, the religious mythology that has dominated Greek thought and out of which the Sophists rose, presenting a relativistic, empirical philosophy on the basis of which no distinction between truth and opinion could be made. I mentioned the Platonic attempt at finding such an objective position through the idos, the ideal, and the essence of things that is the real reality behind the apparent reality that we perceive with our senses. Aristotle uses a different basic concept that is telos, that is to say, the innate purpose that a particular living thing has. I have given you the example of the acorn in which the oak teleologically is preformed and the acorn achieves its realization, its purpose in life, when it has become an oak. And so in every living being, in men and beasts, there is a teleological principle that gives meaning to his life, and toward the fulfillment, the realization to which he aspires. And so, when Aristotle deals with politics, he asks himself what is the telos of man? How can he achieve this purpose for the sake of which he exists?

Now, this teleological principle is quite obvious in the first sentence of *The Politics*: "Every state is a community of some kind and every community is established with a view to some good." That is to say, any social organism has a teleological principle that ties it together and from which it receives its

---

13. This section begins a new day of lectures, September 26, 1970. Because the themes have not changed, I have left it as a continuation of the previous section.

distinctive characteristics. So the state is a social organism, a social phenomenon like others. But then the question arises, what is the difference between the state and the other social organisms, such as the family and so forth? And Aristotle concludes that the state or the political community is the highest community and embraces all the rest. Since it is the highest, it aspires to a good that is superior to the good that the other associations pursue; it is the highest good. And this distinction between the state and other social organisms is not quantitative but qualitative. Man cannot achieve his telos outside the state. So the state is essential for the individual's ability to achieve his purpose in life. Without the state he could not do it.

This conception is obviously at odds with both the liberal and the Marxist conception of the state. For nineteenth-century liberalism the state was a nuisance whose activities had to be limited as much as possible. As Pope put it: "That government is best that governs least."[14] So you get in nineteenth-century liberalism the conception of the night-watchman state, the state that keeps the traffic moving, as we would say today, that sees to it that one individual respects the freedom of the other individual and vice versa, that criminal laws are enforced. But the state according to nineteenth-century liberalism has minimal functions; it is simply a kind of enlarged police enterprise. It certainly has nothing to do in a positive way with the achievement of the ends of the individual and certainly it is not essential; it is not indispensable to the achievement of the individual's aims.

If you look at Marxism, you find the state defined again in quite different terms from Aristotle. Because according to Marx the state is the executive committee of the ruling class. It is the organization of violence that prevents the majority of exploited individuals from overthrowing the exploiting minority. In other words, the justification of the state, according to Marx, lies in the class structure of society. One small minority class that governs can govern only through violence and the state provides the instruments of violence. This being so, in a classless society, the state can wither away, as Engels put it, because it has no function to perform. Being the organization of violence for the purpose of keeping the exploiting minority (the ruling class) in power, once classes have disappeared, the state disappears with them. So you have here an entirely different conception of the state and its relationship to the individual.

Aristotle, an individual who leaves the state and establishes a commune for himself and like-minded individuals or goes back to the soil and wants nothing to do with the state, is (as the Greek word has it) an *idiotes*, which we call today an idiot. In the original Greek sense this means somebody who only cares for himself. *Idios*, what belongs to himself, is a selfish creature who cannot achieve his ends in life, who cannot materialize his telos because he does not participate in

---

14. This quote is generally attributed to either Thomas Paine or Thomas Jefferson. It is unclear if the error is Morgenthau's or the original transcriber of his tapes. It may also be the case that Alexander Pope (1688–1744) is correct here, although I am not sure of this. I am grateful to John Tessitore for help on this point.

the life of the state. So the participation in the life of the state is an indispensable prerequisite for the individual's achievement of his destiny in life.

The method that Aristotle uses to develop the objective necessity of the state is a method typical for him. As he states in *The Politics*, "As in other departments of science, so in politics, the compound should always be resolved into the simple elements or at least parts of the whole. We must therefore look at the elements of which the state is composed in order that we may see in what the different kinds of rule differ from one another, and whether any scientific result can be obtained about each of them." In other words, in order to prove the uniqueness of the state and its highest nature, its being the highest human community, it is necessary to dissolve the state into its constitutive components. And so he starts out by saying, "In the first place there must be a union of those who cannot exist without each other." This is the basis for any stable society. This we find, of course, in the family, because the family is not an artificial invention but for certain higher elements as well as for man, the family is the precondition for the continuation of the race.

It is, of course, not necessary that the people who form a family are conscious of this telos. The very fact that they form it is the objective manifestation of a telos that they consciously or unconsciously serve. The survival of the race is the fundamental justification, the telos of all social associations of which, of course, the family is the most natural, the most elemental. He makes a similar statement with regard to slavery, and he justifies slavery by again saying not so much that the masters need the slaves but the slaves need the master. In other words, nature has distinguished between male and female and, according to Aristotle, also has distinguished between master and slave. So the slave has certain natural characteristics—or, if you wish, certain natural deficiencies—that make it necessary for him, in order to survive and achieve his telos, that he submit himself to the will of a master who has rational faculties to take care of himself and of the slaves. So you have here a principle of extreme natural inequality that justifies slavery. Indeed, if there were such an extreme inequality foreordained by nature among different types of people, as there is, for instance, between grownups and children, slavery would be justified in the interest of the slaves as the exercise of authority by somebody in the family is justified by the temporary deficiency of the children.

Once a number of families exist and several families enter into an association and aim at something more than the supply of daily needs, the first society to be formed is a village. And from this Aristotle derives the necessity of a monarchical form of government because a village, this colony of families, must have a ruler. And the ruler was in the Hellenic states originally the king. Every family, he says, is ruled by the eldest; and therefore in the colony of the families, the kingly form of government prevailed because they were of the same plot. This is again exposed to the same historical argument, that this was so in Greece but is not necessarily so and was different elsewhere. Now, when several villages are united in a single complete community large enough to be nearly or quite self-sufficient, the state comes into existence, "originating in the bare needs of life and continuing in existence for the sake of a good life."

Here Aristotle makes a very important distinction. The telos of the family is the *bare life*, the physical survival of its members. This is, of course, the function that the family performs among higher animals, apes, and so forth. But the state has a different function: Its telos is to provide the *good life*, and this, of course, is a crucial distinction. The telos of the state is not just to ensure the bare survival of the citizens; it is not only life as such that the state must preserve, but liberty and the pursuit of happiness, that is, the good life. And in the statement of the Declaration of Independence—"life, liberty, and the pursuit of happiness"—you have the two factors that Aristotle distinguishes: life per se, sheer survival in the Hobbesian sense; and the good life, which is composed, according to the Declaration of Independence, of liberty and the pursuit of happiness.

Societies that ants or bees or monkeys form are incomplete or lower types of associations from the state because, as it were, the animals are lower types than man is. What distinguishes man, what exalts man over the animals is the gift of speech because it is the gift of speech that makes man into a moral being who can tell just from unjust and can, therefore, infuse the state with certain moral values, especially with the idea of justice.

In any event, I would accept Aristotle's statement that the gift of speech is essential to abstract thought and to abstract judgments. Aristotle, who is very shrewd, makes this point right away and says it is the distinction between animals and man. "And whereas mere voice is but an indication of pleasure or pain and is, therefore, found in other animals, the power of speech is intended to set forth the expedient end the inexpedient and, therefore, likewise the just and the unjust." You see, it is the just and the unjust, the abstract moral judgments; it is also the ability of practical judgment that requires speech. Is it expedient to pursue this kind of policy? Or is it not expedient?

This is a question that you could, of course, decide by physical reactions if it were simply a question of whether you should be beaten over the head or not beaten over the head; or if the dog should be kicked or should not be kicked. But if you deal with state policies in our sense of certain people who act for the whole community, set out to do certain things, then the question arises, Is it sound and right for them to do those things or should they rather do other things? You cannot pass judgment on the expediency of those actions without words, without the verbal faculty. I think Aristotle is right when he makes this basic distinction between animals and man. It is characteristic of man that he alone has any sense of good and evil, of just and unjust, and the like; and the association of living beings who have this sense makes a family and a state.

Now Aristotle tells us:

The state is by nature clearly prior to the family, to the individual, since the whole is of necessity prior to the part. For example, if the whole body be destroyed, there will be no foot or hand except in an equivocal sense when we might speak of a stone hand, for when destroyed, the hand will be no better than that. But things are defined by their working and power and we ought not say that they are the same when they no longer have the proper quality, but only that they have the same name. The proof that the state is the creation of nature and prior to the individual is that the individual, when isolated, is not self-sufficing and therefore is like a part in relation to the whole. But he who is unable to live in society and who has no need because he is sufficient for himself must be either a beast or a god. He is no part of the state.[15]

Here is the source of a whole tradition of political philosophy, sometimes called the organic tradition of political philosophy, which has been most fully developed by Thomas Aquinas and some Catholic writers and which has had a certain theoretical and intellectual impact upon Fascism, especially in Italy and Spain and Portugal, in the form of the corporate state. The assumption is that the state is the primordial phenomenon, that the state is like the body, and the individuals are like members of the body and the state is organized in a perfectly rational way so that each member of the state performs certain necessary functions that are attuned to functions of all the other members. So that in the ideal corporate state, you have a replica of the human body in which nothing is wasted, everything has its purpose and, for that reason, the state functions well. This theory, this doctrine is, of course, a very powerful justification and ideology of the *status quo*. Reform, let us speak of evolution, within such a state is a sickness, is a disease, like the changes in the functions of the different parts of the body are the symptoms of a disease.

In other words, you assume a healthy political organism in which everybody performs a particular function and does not try to perform another one. His telos is to perform the particular function that is assigned to him, to perfection. And when all do that, you have a perfect state. And anybody who falls down on the job, or somebody who aspires to a different position, to a different function within this Commonwealth, is a disturbing, sick element that has to be eliminated. Those are the philosophic implications of the corporate state.

The political implications are that the philosophy becomes an ideology of the *status quo* and a justification and rationalization, more particularly, of a powerful state because somebody has to keep, as it were, the lower classes in their place; the lower classes who naturally aspire to better their lot, or ambitious politicians or economic leaders who want to move up on the social, economic, and political ladder. The state, the government, then imposes its will upon the individuals within the state, seeing to it that they perform their functions and that they don't try to upset the apple cart by aspiring to different functions or trying to change the functions as they exist. So the idea of the corporate state, which has frequently been suggested as the remedy to our contemporary ills, leads of necessity to the establishment of a strong, if not totalitarian state. And if you take it literally, it is bound to lead to a totalitarian state because somebody has to keep recalcitrant individuals in line.

---

15. Book 1, Chapter 2, p. 1253920–30.

CHAPTER 2

Equality to Freedom

Today we shall discuss the Aristotelian conception of slavery and women, a specific case of the general problem of political inequality. Aristotle obviously is convinced that there exists an inequality of men by nature that must be reflected in the constitution of the state. In other words, men are not only unequal in certain respects—physical, intellectual, and emotional—but also Aristotle maintains that there are by nature people who must rule and that, by nature, people who must be ruled. Those who are by nature the subject of others are slaves or deprived of their political rights. On what principle does Aristotle base this sharp distinction between masters by nature and slaves by nature? How do you find out—by what criteria do you find out—who is born to rule and who is to be ruled?

It has to do with the ability of the individual to rule himself. The ruler has certain rational faculties, which are much more than intellectual faculties, to rule himself, his passions, his destructive tendencies, as you would say today. For this reason he can rule others, but the majority who are destined to be ruled are lacking in this rational faculty by which their passions can be mastered. What is the modern concept of political inequality as it was manifested in many countries in Europe where the franchise was limited? Why was the franchise limited to property holders in Great Britain up to the Reform Acts? Why was it, for instance, in Prussia that the right to vote depended upon property until 1919? During the First World War there was a great debate in the Prussian Parliament about the abolition of the so-called three-class electoral system. The electorate was divided into three classes. A member of each class had a number of votes on the basis of his holding property. If he didn't hold property, he belonged to the lowest class, and women had no right to vote at all.

This section includes seminars from November 6 and 13, 1970, and January 8, 1971.

In other words, the good judgment that is necessary for running political affairs is more likely to be present in property holders who have also a stake in the state. It is not the rabble, which really does not care since it has nothing to lose. The property holder has something to lose, and for this reason he will make judicious use of his political power. What about slavery in this country or in any other country? The problem is never raised in philosophic terms. In this country what was the philosophic basis of slavery?

It was simply this: Blacks were a lower-caste people in Aristotelian terms. Southern aristocrats quoted Aristotle and the Bible in order to show that a black man by nature was inferior to the white man and could not take care of his affairs. The paternalistic conception of the justification of slavery was based upon the Aristotelian principle; that is, to take good care of the slave was regarded as a moral principle. The master took good care of the slave because the slave couldn't take care of himself. So you have here an assimilation of the relationship between a father and child. As a child cannot take care of himself, so the father does what the child cannot do. As a slave cannot take care of himself, the master does for him.

You had until recently many southerners who prided themselves in their amicable and mutually beneficial relations between the whites and the blacks, assuming that this relationship was best for both those concerned. It was in the interest of the blacks and it was in the interest of the whites. If you look at the justification for colonialism in Great Britain you find a very similar conception. If you read for instance the essay of John Stuart Mill on nonintervention, you'll find it the most fantastic ideological justification of British policy.[1] It is fantastic because it comes from the pen of a genius, of an unusually intelligent man. Mill makes a point that Britain has never interfered in the affairs of other nations, and when it has as in the case of India, it was only for the good of the barbarians. Here were again people who could not take care of their own affairs and were in a semi-barbaric state. The British would bring the enlightened principles of human life to those disadvantaged barbarians.

You have the same in the Spanish justification in the colonization of the Western Hemisphere. The Spaniards thought that they had a positive moral duty to bring the blessings of Christianity to the heathens; to convert the heathens was in the interest of the heathens themselves because it was beneficial for their salvation. Those who refused to accept the superior religion of the whites were justly put to the sword because they were beyond redemption. They were really useless beings who happened to appear in the form of human beings.

Consider also in our own history the justification of the annexation of the Philippines. In a speech that Senator Beveridge[2] of Indiana made in the Senate in

---

1. J. S. Mill, "A Few Words on Non-Intervention," in *The Collected Works of J. S. Mill*, vol. 21 (Toronto: University of Toronto Publishing, 1988).

2. Senator Albert J. Beveridge (1862–1927) of Indiana, one of the leading proponents of the economic and moral benefits of colonialism in the late nineteenth and early twentieth centuries.

order to justify the annexation of the Philippines, he said we must bring the blessings of Western civilization to our little brown brothers for whom Christ also died. You have again the same paternalistic conception of the relations between master and slave or between the colonial power and the colonized people; that the rule of the master, the white man, is not justified in terms of the good of the white man, but in terms of the moral duty that the white man as a master has toward the slave or the colony. It is for the betterment of the life of the slave or the colonized people that the rule of the master or the colonial power must be put into practice.

Returning to the question of slavery, to what extent really was the slavery in the South insofar as its economic aspects were concerned different from slavery in Athens? I would guess that the situations were very similar. The slaves would do the manual labor whatever it might be and thereby free the masters from the drudgery, enabling them to lead the lives of gentlemen of leisure, cultivating things of the mind. I don't see any basic difference between the two situations. Industry under the conditions of slavery was minimal, if it existed at all. The slave can really not be used for higher industrial purposes because for that purpose you need some knowledge, the development of intellectual faculties. In our society today the functionally illiterate are unemployable because they cannot read instructions. It's as simple as that. Furthermore, they haven't been accustomed to the discipline and at least the elementary type of initiative that is indispensable—and also the understanding of certain basic technical operations, which are indispensable for modern industrial production. I would not think there is any noticeable difference between the function the slave performed in the Southern society and that which he performed in Athens. The Aristotelian conception covers both situations.

Now how does Aristotle define who is a slave? His definition of a slave is someone who is a slave. This really doesn't tell us anything. Somebody decides who is to be a natural slave. The decision is made probably on the basis of a very superficial examination of his rational faculties. What you get then is a class structure in which certain people are relegated to the position of slavery on the basis of the opinion of the master class. There was of course inherited slavery; the son of a slave is a slave. How the original decision was made is an open question. It is possible that the Athenians conquered Athens, found an indigenous population, and reduced them to slaves.

In regard to slavery, Aristotle makes the distinction between natural slaves and legal slaves. And of course with regard to legal slaves you haven't any problem, because certain people were either conquered or they became indebted to some creditor, and legally were stamped as slaves. This doesn't mean anything with regard to their nature. You change the legal status and the man is free again. But the real problems arise of course with regard to the natural slaves. How a natural slave rises to the position in which it is justified to free him and to make him a free man is of the same order of magnitude as the question concerning slavery itself. By what criterion are you going to determine in the original situation who is supposed to be a slave and who is not? The question arises again once the institution of slavery is established with regard to the freedom of the slaves. At what point has a slave acquired the rational faculties that justify his liberation? There is no objective criterion. Aristotle assumes that this becomes so obvious in one way or the other, either by his lack of rational faculties or his acquisition of rational faculties, that it will be easy to decide who is who.

Some would object to this reasoning. The fact that he has the potential to acquire these rational faculties would refute the principle that there is such a thing as a natural slave because the natural slave has the potential not to be a slave.

This is rebutted by the claim that human nature is malleable and can develop. Like a retarded child, it can acquire certain mental faculties. I would not say there is a contradiction. There would be a contradiction only if you were to assume that human nature is fixed once and forever and will be inherited in its fixed and immutable state. This is not what Aristotle believes. Aristotle believes that there is development, and a slave who today has not the rational faculties sufficient for being a free man may acquire these rational faculties, or his children or his grandchildren, and so forth. The basic issue to which the Aristotelian argument in favor of slavery gives rise is of course the proper issue of political inequality.

Let me say a word about the position of women. Here it becomes clearer what Aristotle has in mind in general. He says women are naturally inferior to men. They are different from men because they perform different functions—procreation and taking care of the family. They are of such a nature as to require the imposition of male mastery over the women and over the family. So it is a natural distinction that leads to this inferiority of women because of their performance of specific functions that are inferior to the functions that the head of the household, the man, must perform. You have here a clear case of a cultural conditioning—a particular aspect of Athenian culture is erected into an absolute principle of philosophy.

We all share certain cultural presumptions about gender. Consider the following example: A father and his daughter are in a car accident. The daughter is brought to the hospital. The doctor takes one look at her and says, "I cannot treat that patient. That patient is my daughter." What is the solution to the riddle? The doctor is the mother of that girl. It is a very embarrassing discovery to me—how we are culturally conditioned. We live in a man's world and cannot imagine that a doctor could be a woman. I have asked this question of 100 people, and only three have known the answer. I was asked that question at a convention by the women's organization of political science who wanted to know whether they could support me. I flunked and my opponent flunked too, so they took another look and said I was probably better than the opponent and they endorsed me.

It shows how enormous those cultural blinders are that allow us only to see certain things and not other things. This is obvious in Aristotle as well. The real profound and important question that his discussion of slavery raises is the problem of political inequality. It is obvious that people are different, not only in a great number of respects irrelevant to politics, but also with regard to politics. Some people have what we call political know-how. They are extremely adept at acquiring power and using it, and others are not. The ones who are adept at acquiring power and using it are a small minority. If one takes a professional point of view of politics, one would arrive at the conclusion that an aristocratic government is really the best government because it is composed of a small elite of people who know how to govern, who know their business. In a democracy with general suffrage, you have no guarantee that the people who know how to govern, who know their job as politicians and statesmen are put in the position of power. You have only to look at our government to see how true it is.

From a strictly professional, pragmatic point of view there is something to be said in favor of the Aristotelian conception of a political society. In the same way in which we allow only certain people who have proven their qualifications to be doctors or lawyers or dentists or accountants, one could argue with Aristotle that only the people who know how to govern, who know the business of politics, ought to be put in the position of political power. The ultimate extension of this is the Platonic conception of the philosopher king. The philosopher who is supposed to know everything on a very profound level of the state ought to be the king who reigns supreme. Aristotle remains completely in this Platonic condition. Obviously there must be another argument that justifies our egalitarian conception of politics. We are not just ignorant or misguided that we assume that everybody ought to vote, and that everybody should have a chance to be elected to political office. What is the argument in favor of our egalitarianism?

One argument in favor of our egalitarianism is that all men are endowed with certain rational faculties to a greater or lesser extent. No large minority is so completely devoid of rational faculties they would rather be put in the position of slavery or at least to be disenfranchised. There is, however, a still more important argument. This argument developed directly out of the Greek tradition. What intellectual movement of ancient times is completely opposed to the Aristotelian distinction?

The answer is Stoic relativism. In other words, since relativism assumes that there is no absolute truth, at least no absolute truth recognizable or intelligible by man, you have to give all groups within the state an equal chance to prove their truth. I should put it this way: You have to put the different truths that fight with each other to the scrutiny of the electorate, and then the majority will decide which interest it will accept and ask the government to pursue. This is the Holmes conception of relativism. Mr. Justice Holmes[3] has said he knows only of one test to determine the quality of the law, and that is what the crowd wants. Of course, this is not an extremely elevated conception of equality, but it points to one symbol, an obvious test, and that is that since there are a multiplicity of interests within a given society, and many of those interests claim that they have a majority

---

3. Oliver Wendell Holmes (1841–1935) served as associate justice of the U.S. Supreme Court from 1902 to 1932. He was known for his belief that even if the people are wrong, as expressed in their legislature, they deserve the laws those legislators make.

behind them and they are the legitimate majority, you need a mechanical, peaceful, and orderly way to determine this claim. That is majority rule, based on the equality of all interests to compete for recognition. Mr. Justice Holmes says that the competition of the marketplace will lead to the discovery of truth in the democratic sense; that there is an antecedent of this pragmatic relativistic concept that leads to equality. There is another much more profound concept that has dominated the modern world and which grew directly from the Hellenistic version of Aristotelian philosophy.

I am, incidentally, not speaking here of the old inner contradiction of relativism: If all truths are relative, then the truth of relativism is relative too. The ancient rhetoricians used to play around with this. What is the answer to that argument? The argument is in itself superficially cogent: If all truths are relative, according to relativism, then the truth of relativism is relative too. It cannot be accepted as an absolute principle. If everything is relative the truth of relativism is relative too. What about the answer to that riddle?

You have here a juxtaposition of a procedural truth. All truths are relative. It is not a substantive statement about anything in particular. It is simply an utterance concerning the quality, the epistemological quality of different substantive principles, but is not in itself a substantive principle, so the relativistic argument doesn't apply to it. But we still haven't found the most profound, the most historical, most consequential principle upon which modern egalitarianism is based.

Where is the source of modern egalitarianism, in particular the American egalitarianism from which the opposition to slavery originally emanated? The answer is religion, which leads to the idea that all men are created in the image of God. It is absolutely incompatible with slavery. If all men are the children of God, they are equal in the sight of God. Here is the real philosophic and theological source of modern egalitarianism. How does the Declaration of Independence start? With the phrase that "all men are created equal" and the equality is not argued in terms of biology or psychology, but on the basis of the laws of nature and of nature's God. What is the basic source of the opposition to slavery in this country and later the movements for equal rights not only on the statue books but also in reality? On the basis of what is essentially a secularized religious tradition, we simply do not believe in the essential inequality of man with regard to civil or political rights. We all recognize the inequality. There are people who have even argued that in certain respects blacks are inferior to whites intellectually, but this is irrelevant in terms of the basic proposition that the essential equality of man as man, if you want to avoid the theological argument, transcends all their inequalities.

True, some interpreted this to mean, say, only for Christians, but not savages, for instance. But you have to distinguish between the intrinsic meaning of the principle and its application in practice. The principle itself means what it says: All men are created equal. And not by some chance but by the objective laws by which the universe is constituted. That in practice we have violated this basic principle is an entirely different matter. You take a man like Jefferson who, because he believed in this principle in the Declaration of Independence, tried to bring his slaves to a point where they could be freed because they could take care of themselves. I think here is the ultimate source of modern equality that is of course utterly at variance with the Aristotelian conception. Politically speaking, this doctrine injected into the Hellenistic world two thousand years ago was political and social dynamite. All of a sudden Christianity told the slaves you are not inferior in the eyes of God. (Certain Christians would hold, as they had in the South 150 years ago, that while they may be equal in the sight of God, they are still unequal in empirical terms and therefore have to be treated as such.) Once you introduce this principle into the political dialogue, you certainly could interpret it as being in opposition to aristocratic rule, slavery, and so forth. What the principle of equality means in practice is a different question, but the principle itself was of enormous consequence because it could be interpreted (and was then later interpreted, and was originally also interpreted up to a certain point) in terms of the equality of all men in political terms—and certainly as an argument against slavery. It was circumvented by saying, yes, the slaves are equal to us, but they are not yet capable of making good use of that equality. For this reason we have to take care of them, keep them in slavery. But once you had this principle on the agenda of mankind, it was inevitable that sooner or later it would be interpreted in the modern egalitarian way.

The Christian conception of equality before God was in complete conflict with Aristotle's state. You had this conflict between two different conceptions very clearly in the Spanish colonies in Latin America. The great conquistadores went there, robbed, plundered, and killed without discrimination. The Spanish king sent orders—and the Jesuits put those orders into practice on their own—regarding the Indians as men, and therefore endowed with the same equality. They were heathens or blind men or men who had not developed what Aristotle called their telos to the full because they had not seen the light of salvation. Make them accept that light, transform them to Christians, and they will be treated on equal terms with other Christians.

I am speaking here of the Christian principle. While it is also organic based on the theory of Aristotle, it allows for what you call today "upward mobility." There will always be a class of inferior people, the lower classes that perform the functions appropriate to the lower classes. But there is a possibility for a member of the lower class to rise in the social hierarchy by proving that he can perform the functions that are appropriate to a higher class. I should say that this principle that there is a lower class that by nature is precluded from rising in the social pyramid, and that is by nature reduced to menial labor or unemployment in our time, has been most forcefully presented by Professor Banfield of Harvard in his recent book *The Unheavenly City*.[4] It simply says you can't improve upon the lot of the lower classes; they are lower by nature or by social necessity, and there will always be a lower class, and let's face it. This is a sociological application of

---

4. Edward C. Banfield, *The Unheavenly City: The Nature and Future of Our Urban Crisis* (Boston: Little, Brown Co., 1970).

the basic principle that those people hold those views, engage in those practices, of a naturally lower type than the higher classes. It is essentially the same principle of inequality, however you argue the case; and of course in our time you argue it in behaviorist and sociological terms. But you have to push the argument one step back and ask yourself why are they the way they are? What makes them a lower class that in its activities is inferior to the higher classes? Why are there then capitalists or barons of industry who evidently by nature are destined to play a dominant, creative, guiding role in the affairs of society? Why are there others like the lower classes that are incapable of performing such tasks? Even more important, why must they always be with us, because this is the Banfield argument. You can increase the number of social works threefold and add billions of dollars to the poverty program and in the end you will still have that lower class.

Banfield believes in the inevitability of the lower class. As people used to say in times past, the poor will always be with us. This is a philosophic elaboration of this principle. Now Aristotle says simply there are certain people who, if you would subject them to a number of tests, would turn out to be incapable of governing themselves, taking care of their interests. It is not necessarily genetic; those people are simply around. Aristotle says, and I think Banfield says, that they'll always be around. You might be able to rescue this particular group of lower classes, but another lower class will then emerge. Banfield would say there are people who are by nature—or by culture, if you wish—so improvident that even in an economy of plenty, they would not be able to take care of their affairs. They would simply drink themselves to death or buy lottery tickets, or bet on the horses, or whatever you do if you are irresponsible and have a lot of money.

Banfield, whom I know very well, was a colleague of mine for a long time in Chicago. Banfield is a conservative. He cannot believe in any other social system except the one we have. Since this system is enormously stable and powerful, he assumes it will last as long as one wants to look in the future. Then it follows also that there must always be a class of people who are improvident and incapable of making a go of it. You might even say that this is so in a non-capitalistic country. In the Soviet Union those people are put into insane asylums or labor camps. They are removed by force from society and are put into a situation where they are compelled to lead a productive life in an artificial society, which is the concentration camp or the labor camp, prison or insane asylum, which are all societies for the purpose of removing certain elements from the official society, which for one reason or another this society does not want to cope with. Consider insane asylums, where, without any doubt, the commitment of a man as being insane is in a good measure a reflection of a particular culture that cannot tolerate a certain behavior.

For instance, I had a friend who was a brilliant sociologist who was confined to the State Hospital in Peoria, Illinois, for I think eleven years. He did not fit into this particular society; he was an impossible fellow in terms of our society. He was a pain in the neck. Society tolerates such a fellow up to a certain point, but if he acts in what we call a "strange way," then we put him away. He became cured after eleven years; he was exactly as he was before, but since he had been reduced almost to a vegetable, he would no longer be obnoxious to society.[5]

In the Soviet Union you have a simple situation. Since the Soviet Union claims a monopoly on truth and virtue, anybody who denies that claim must be out of his mind. If you believe that you have a monopoly of truth and virtue, then anybody who dissents from your point of view is either a criminal or crazy. For this reason it is only a relativistic political society such as ours, at least within certain limits, that is capable of tolerating dissent. For this reason Mr. Justice Holmes can say that the competition of the marketplace will determine the truth. No man dedicated to an otherworldly religion that has come to him through divine revelation, or a political absolutist could say that the truth will be determined by the competition of the market. For the Soviet Union the truth is determined by the Politburo, which is in a sense the College of Cardinals that interprets the Holy Scriptures of Marx and Lenin to concrete situations. Who denies this is either a Fascist beast, a criminal, or crazy.

In the United States, the limits allowed by the system are of course much broader. In other words, you have a variety of opinions that are still allowed in our society. The opposite philosophies—the philosophy of relativism—are most cogently expressed by Oliver Cromwell. Cromwell's statement is the Scottish Presbyterian's: "I beseech you by the bowels of Christ, is it possible that you can be mistaken?" This is the exact opposite of the religious intolerance or the political intolerance that assumes a monopoly on truth and virtue. Truth's assumption compels the Soviets to outlaw as either the criminal or insane all divergent opinions. If you have this absolutistic point of view, you arrive at the conclusion that Soviet officials have argued from time and time again that their press is the only one that is free. It is the only press that reports only the truth. Our press is degenerate, as Russians have told me many times. A press that is allowed to propagate lies is a degenerate, corrupt press. This is perfectly logical once you start with the assumption from which any absolutistic philosophy argues.

What is the real problem with regard to egalitarianism in the modern sense is that you have to decide in what respects equality is politically relevant, to what extent inequalities are not. For a long time, until the beginning of the century, political equality did not apply to women. Women were regarded to be of such an unequal nature to man that this inequality would lead to their disenfranchisement. In other words, that women are different from men is obvious, a biological fact. That they are also emotionally different from men is a demonstrable fact. The real question is, are those differences politically relevant, and if they are, in what respect?

The contemporary position is that these differences are politically irrelevant, and therefore women ought to have the same political rights as men. You have the same issue with regard to color. There has been a time, not so long ago, when color

---

5. According to Mitchell Rologus, a Morgenthau expert, Morgenthau's reference here is to the sociologist Gustav Ichheiser (1897–1969).

was an obvious difference that was regarded to be politically relevant. That there is a difference in color amongst different human beings is obvious. But then the question arises, are the differences in the color of the skin politically relevant? Again there has been a long tradition that maintains the relevance of that distinction. We don't regard it as relevant anymore. Or property—the possession of property was regarded for a long time as a difference that was politically relevant—and only property holders would have the franchise. Or that there is a difference between members of aristocratic families brought up within a particular aristocratic environment is also obvious. Is this aristocratic character of certain people politically relevant? There was again a time where it was, where somebody who was not of the nobility could not get a job in the foreign office or in the army, and so forth.

Or take religion. Religion was regarded as relevant for a long time: disenfranchisement of Catholics in Great Britain, of Jews in most countries. The real issue of what you call political equality lies in our determination as to what difference— and of course there are a multitude of differences among human beings—is politically relevant. We take it for granted that age is relevant for the acquisition of political rights. We don't give babies the franchise or ten-year-olds, not fifteen-year-olds. Our opinion as to what is relevant and not relevant in the obvious differences among human beings is determined by our culture or by political interests. It cannot be objectively, philosophically determined in any unambiguous way. Of course we can say that only people who have a certain rational faculty should be allowed to vote, so we withdraw the vote from certain types of criminals who have shown their asocial character in a consistent way. We deprive certain insane people from the vote because they are not supposed to have the rational faculty necessary to make a rational distinction with their vote.

Frequently those principles are violated either for better or for worse. In the case of color, they are violated for worse. But you might say when it comes to opening up the aristocracy to certain bourgeoisie elements that really should not be there, the distinction becomes blurred. You violate again the aristocratic principle of inequality by opening the gates to a certain influx of commoners, in the way that Great Britain has renewed the dynamics of its aristocratic society. On the other hand, you can have the most extreme applications of the principal of inequality on the basis of religion. Here you have a criterion, which is very clear, and you can exclude certain people from political functions by pointing to the wrong religion they hold. On the other hand, a change of religion will automatically eliminate the handicap. Take for instance the famous statement of Henry II of France that Paris is worth a Mass. As a Protestant, he does not have a chance; he becomes a Catholic and everything is all right.

The modern racial distinctions or other ethnic characteristics are much more difficult to overcome than the religious. For the religious it was simple; change your religion and you're all right. But you can't change your color or your ethnic origins. The disabilities today in terms of political equality are much more difficult to overcome than were the religious or aristocratic ones.

Let me give you an example of the manipulation of religion as a political instrument that can prevent the application of equality in practice. There was before the First World War a German Jew by the name of Ballin, who was one of the most prominent Jews in Germany, a personal friend of the Kaiser, the head of the Hamburg-America line, and one of the great figures in Germany. He committed suicide on November 9, 1918, when the German Reich collapsed. This man married a Christian widow who had a daughter from the first marriage, which was completely Christian. This daughter fell in love with an officer of the German navy, and the officer had to renounce his commission in order to marry her. There was no ethnic problem at all. There was only a very remote religious problem in that her stepfather was Jewish, which was sufficient to ruin the career of her future husband because of the religious connotations. If Ballin had allowed himself to be baptized—he was not a practicing Jew at all; he just happened to be the son of Jewish parents—and had embraced Christianity, nobody would have raised any questions.[6]

The same was true with regard to full professorships. Before the First World War a Jew could not become a full professor. Men like Simmel, the great sociologist, reached a level of assistant professor, and so did Freud.[7] If Simmel or Freud had been baptized, they would have become full professors in no time. The religious infringement upon equality is much more easily remediable than many others, because you merely change your religion and you are right in terms of the political preferences of a particular society.

You have another concept of equality that is not political but legal, and that is comprised in the statement, "equality before the law." That is to say, the law should not discriminate against you on the basis of criteria that are not relevant to the law itself. You cannot have complete equality before the law because your position vis-à-vis the law will differ from the position of others. You may have defaulted upon a payment of your car and the dealer wants to repossess the car. The same may be true of somebody else. You have real property and the other person does not, so you can take a mortgage on your property and pay the dealer and the law will recognize this. The other person cannot. You have inequality that is relevant to the legal situation, and that the law recognizes.

Again you come up against the problem I have discussed before: What kind of differences are relevant in legal terms? Take, for instance, the distinction the law makes between men and women concerning the custodianship of children or the payment of alimony in cases of divorce. In those cases the law deals with the husband in an entirely different way from the way it deals with the woman. It discriminates between the two sexes. The question arises: Is this discrimination legally valid? In other words, is this discrimination, this denial of equality, the

---

6. Albert Ballin (1857–1918) was a successful German business leader in Hamburg and founder of the Hamburg-Amerikanische Packetfahrt-Actiengesellschaft, which became known as Hapag, a shipping line that catered primarily to emigrants from Germany to the United States. He was known as the only Jewish friend of Kaiser Wilhelm II.

7. George Simmel (1858–1918), the German sociologist, and Sigmund Freud (1856–1939), the founder of modern psychology.

result of certain legally irrelevant differences or is it arbitrary in that it discriminates between men and women on the basis of criteria that are not legally relevant? This question is coming up right now before the court, because the alimony
laws have been challenged on the basis that they are very much in favor of the
wife to the detriment of the husband. The question has been raised that this is a violation of the principle of equality. The question is, is it? The answer to the question hinges on whether the discriminatory aspects of the law are legally relevant
in that they refer to different legal situations and different legal interests or
whether they are arbitrary, capricious, and therefore must be abolished.

This question came up historically over seventy years ago when certain states
passed laws against the employment of children and setting limitations upon the
working hours of women. The argument was made that this is discriminatory.
There is no reason in law for this violation of equality and therefore the laws are
null. In the famous case of *Miller v. Oregon* this question came up.[8] In this case
the court decided that a law limiting the working hours of women was discriminatory and a violation of the freedom of contract. Our conception of equality is
determined by certain ethical and cultural preconceptions that are subject to
change in time. Look at the position of women today and compare it with what it
was only fifty years ago. Fifty years ago it was generally agreed that women
should not vote. They had no rights to full citizenship because of their biological
differences. Today we are of the opinion that those biological differences are not
relevant in political terms and therefore women should have political equality
with men.

In former periods of history it was regarded as extraordinary if a woman
would go out and earn a living; it was regarded as eccentric and was a negative
reflection on the husband or the parents who couldn't afford to support her. But
the basic problem remains: What is politically relevant and what is not? We
say today an eighteen-year-old has now reached a state of intellectual maturity,
of the development of his rational faculties that is as great as was formerly attributed to the twenty-one-year-old. For this reason, we can reduce the time limit
from twenty-one years to eighteen years for a young person to have the right to
vote. It is possible that fifty years from now, twenty years from now, education
will have made such progress that fifteen- or sixteen-years-old is enough. This is
culturally conditioned, but what remains is a basic problem. What is politically
relevant in view of the actual manifold inequalities in human beings? Equality in
practice is not a mechanical concept. It is a concept that receives its concrete,
substantive meaning from the particular cultural environment within which it
is applied.

For Aristotle the issue of slavery becomes really the issue of political inequality.[9] This is a matter of fundamental importance for us. We assume equality in

---

8. *Frederick L. Miller v. The State of Oregon* (1927).
9. The seminar of November 13, 1970, begins here.

a certain sense, in the political and legal sense. We are aware of the actual inequality of individuals in a number of different respects. Only we assume this inequality in terms of physical ability, intellectual ability, moral characters—those inequalities are irrelevant for politics. This is an assumption that appears within the democratic ethos to be self-evident but which is certainly susceptible to critical analysis. I have already mentioned Professor Banfield's assumption that there is a lower class, a group destined to find by natural qualities that it is precluded from rising in the social scale. To try to ameliorate that fate may be, from a humanitarian point of view, desirable and defensible, but the idea that you can abolish poverty, for instance, by raising the lower class to the level of a middle class is a futile undertaking. By nature those people are destined to remain within the lower class. They are destined to be there because they are lacking in those qualities—moral, intellectual, physical—which go into the making of the middle or higher classes. The issue that Aristotle raises is an obsolete issue in the terms that he poses, that is, in the terms of slavery. In its more general terms, and this is the way Aristotle argues (otherwise he would not spend so much space on slavery), this issue is political inequality—and as such it is a perennial issue of political philosophy.

Aristotle differs in important ways from more modern attempts to differentiate slaves and masters. He focuses on the moral and rational qualities of masters and slaves rather than their physical qualities. Aristotle is too intelligent a man to deny, as for instance the Nazis did, that certain groups of people, the so-called lower races, are devoid of human qualities. As the Germans called it, *Untermenschen*; they are sub-human. They look like humans, but in actuality they aren't. Aristotle does not go to such lengths. He does not deny, and does not intend to deny, that the slaves are human, that they are endowed with some type of moral and rational faculties. But he must at the same time establish the qualitative difference between masters and slaves. He does this by making the point that the slaves participate in a rational principle enough to apprehend, but not to have such a principle. A man so endowed, who participates in rational principle enough to apprehend but not to have such a principle, is a slave by nature. Whereas the lower animals cannot even apprehend a principle, they obey their instincts. Indeed, the use made of slaves and tame animals is not very different. Both with their bodies minister to needs of life. The difference, in other words, between masters and slaves lies in the ability of the slaves to apprehend and the masters to have a rational principle. A slave can understand it, but he cannot act upon it.

This is true of slaves as well as women, according to Aristotle. This is different from the Nazis racial theorists. Aristotle does not see any physical differences between slaves and masters. Nature would like to distinguish between the bodies of free men and slaves, making the one strong for servant labor and the other upright and so forth. It would be very convenient if you took one look at a man and could reliably say he is a slave and he is a master. The Nazis indeed developed a crude and completely untenable racial theory according to which blue-eyed, blond, tall people belonged to the master race and black-haired, small people did not. They started breeding members of the master race by putting the tall, blond, blue-eyed man together with similarly endowed women in breeding places, like horses. The trouble is you can breed horses because what you need are certain physical characteristics. But you can't breed men beyond certain physical characteristics because other qualities besides physical characteristics are required. Nothing corresponds in the physical makeup of a man to his soul and his rational abilities, which according to Aristotle distinguished masters from slaves. So the physical criterion is simply useless.

What is the ultimate reason for Aristotle's distinction between masters and slaves? What is the fundamental argument that Aristotle applies? It is the concept of telos. Some are born to rule as others are born to obey. It is a teleological destiny of certain men to be slaves and others to be rulers. This is of course a static conception in which the destiny of man is predetermined by the way he is born, and there is no escape from this destiny. In the same way some people are born with a musical ear and others without; some people are born color-blind and others with extreme ability to discern shades of color; and so on, some are born for certain purposes and others are born for other purposes. If a man is born a slave, his telos is to be a slave.

This is the argument that has been used for centuries by invoking Aristotle to defend slavery. In the American South, the institution of slavery was based upon the assumption that Negroes are born to be subordinate to whites. The white man is by nature superior to the black man. This is the important ideological thing—that it is to the benefit of the born slave to be ruled by the master for the simple reason that he cannot govern himself, that he doesn't have the faculties to do so, let alone govern others. Therefore, it is in his best interest to be governed by people who are by nature equipped to govern. From this follows the conception of the paternalistic rule that is in the interest of the ruled. Just as children benefit by being ruled by their parents, so the slave benefits from being ruled by the ruler. The ultimate justification, the source of the distinction is in the teleological character of Aristotle's philosophy.

Here one should note that Aristotle has a very static and, from our point of view, quite an erroneous conception of human nature. The idea that men are born in a certain way and must remain completely within the limits of that way is denied by modern psychology and modern experience. In other words, human nature is malleable within certain limits—and certainly there are limits to it. A man with a certain weak physique cannot be formed into a first rate baseball or football player. Or somebody with a certain brain cannot be educated to become another Einstein. But within certain limits human nature is malleable, and this is what Aristotle completely overlooks. Who determines who is the ruler and who is the slave by nature? Of course the ruler does. He is not going to rule according to eternal verities, but according to his interests. Aristotle is essentially a conservative political philosopher. For this reason he became the model of medieval political philosophy of the organic state and for the justification of slavery for political inequality in modern times.

The other basic argument that Aristotle makes and that is in a sense an application of the teleological principle is the analogy with the human individual. The same way in which the soul reigns over the body and reason reigns over the soul, so the master rules over the ruled. The slave, together with women and children, has the same relation to the ruler as the human body has to the soul and to reason. While the rule of the soul is despotic according to Aristotle, the soul rules without limitations, imposes its will upon the body. The rule of reason, however, is constitutional, is discriminating, rational. It keeps the passions of the soul in check. Similarly, you have two types of government—the despotic rule, which imposes its rule with limitations and restraint, and the constitutional rule, which is the rule of law. The telos of the body, the telos of the soul, the telos of reason, are all predetermined and given objectively in nature. The relations between rulers and ruled are similarly given by nature. In consequence, you arrive at the organic philosophy of the state, which is not based upon exploitation, or class distinctions, or the lust for power, but which is in the same way the empirical expression of the natural order of things, as the relations among reason, soul, and body.

What Aristotle completely neglects in this naturalistic account is that the source of politics can be found in certain passions that are completely separate from his idea of the natural order of things. It is obviously necessary to have some kind of "law and order" in the relations among men, except in a society of saints. Because men are in different ways governed by their passions you need a government that keeps those passions in check. What Aristotle does not see is that the people who by some way come to rule over others are also driven by passions that need to be kept in check. The idea of an organic political system is valid in itself as a philosophic proposition, but it is invalidated from the outset by the corruption of power to which the rulers themselves fall victim. Here is really the basic weakness of not only Aristotle's political philosophy, but also of any organic theory of the state.

For instance, consider the concept of the corporate state, which at one time was the official political doctrine of the Catholic Church, a doctrine attributed to Aristotle and St. Augustine and St. Thomas. This doctrine relied on the idea that there exists in the state the same kind of division of labor that exists in the body. Each group of individuals has a natural station, a natural function that they must perform; and out of the harmonious performance of all those functions, an organism arises, harmonious, peaceful, orderly—that is, the state. What that doctrine fails to realize is that while it is true that different groups within the state perform different functions, the assumption of those functions is not necessarily the result of a natural division of labor but of the usurpation by certain powerful groups of the most beneficial and rewarding functions with the state.

If you look at historic governments and their relations to the governed, you would not say that typically those who govern are best qualified to govern and that they are superior in virtue and rational faculties to those who are governed. Lord Bryce in his *The American Commonwealth* has one chapter with the title,

"Why Great Men are Not Elected President of the United States," giving a number of reasons.[10] If you look at our political life today and the quality of the people who rule compared to the qualities of people who are ruled, it would certainly be hazardous to maintain that the best people rule, and the people who are ruled are by nature precluded from doing so; and those who rule are by nature teleologically appointed to rule. That this makes for an organic political commonwealth is political fiction.

The reason this theory arose was that Athenian democracy was decaying in the times of Plato and Aristotle. They tried to find the true principles of government, the application of which would save Athenian democracy. The thinking of all great political philosophers has grown from a certain concrete political situation. The academic idea, which is common among us, is that you sit in your study and you have a list of topics . . . this idea that you speculate about some kind of esoteric political problem that preferably has no relation to political reality is typically academic. But none of the great political philosophers from Amos and Isaiah to Marx and Lenin has ever operated in such a way. All great political thought has arisen from a political crisis. Why did Hobbes write? Why did Machiavelli write? St. Thomas? Plato? Aristotle? Why did Amos and Isaiah and the other Biblical prophets talk about politics? They confronted the King and told him what he had done wrong. It is not by accident that Aristotle was in political exile. Hobbes and Locke were political exiles. So was Marx. Many of them went to jail. You might say that respectable political science is likely to be irrelevant to the great political issues for the very reason that it is "respectable."

Aristotle and Plato wanted to save Athenian democracy. In order to save it, it was not sufficient to give tactical advice—that is, how this court ought to be reformed, that procedure ought to be done differently. This is the difference between Plato and the Sophists; Plato wanted to find the objective truth about matters political, while the Sophists just wanted to reform by some pragmatic way what was wrong in Athens. Both Plato and Aristotle were conservative political philosophers. They wanted to save the established institutions. In order to do this, they had to establish a clear distinction between the rulers and the ruled. *If* you give the ruled the power to participate, you create an element of uncertainty, instability, a dynamic element that runs counter to this basic aim of preserving the institutions of Athens. For this reason, Aristotle, who was a very practical man, realized the possibility of revolution. If the rulers become corrupted, the ruled will rise and overthrow the rulers; this is a fact of political life.

This leads one to consider the fundamental difference between the Aristotelian recognition of the fact of revolution and the post-Christian conception of the right to revolt. The right to revolt implies the right to rule. For Aristotle revolt was a symptom of the general disease of the body politic. Everything was out of joint,

---

10. James Bryce, *The American Commonwealth* (New York: Macmillian, 1922). I assume this is the edition to which Morgenthau refers.

and so even the body would revolt against the soul and against reason. For medieval political philosophy and for American political philosophy the right to revolt was a right inherent in human nature. This could only be a right inherent in human nature if you assume the political equality of man.

For example, Machiavelli was fully aware of the difference between his political philosophy and ancient political philosophy.[11] He conceived of his political philosophy as a frontal attack against the ancients. He said in the preface to *The Prince*, "My purpose is not to tell you what ought to be (this is what Plato and Aristotle and St. Thomas argue). I want to tell you how it is." In other words, what political life is actually like. What you have to do in order to be successful in politics, which is an eminently practical, nonphilosophical attitude. You take the imperfect world as it is and ask, how do you get ahead, what do you have to do not to be killed but to be able to kill, which is the ultimate test of political success throughout most long periods of history.

Violence has been in most periods of history the ultimate arbiter of political conflict. Nothing is more final than violence in politics. Robert Kennedy is not going to run again for any political office. Nixon did. This is the difference. Nixon was defeated time and again and came back. Robert Kennedy was killed and that was the end. We are talking a great deal about violence. Many people talk against it because nobody can really advocate violence as something better than nonviolence. But violence is in the Machiavellian sense, and even in the Aristotelian sense, a fact of political life. The state is based upon violence, even though we don't realize it because it is surrounded by legal safeguards, and is embedded in institutions that have a positive legitimacy. The policeman who hits me over the head with a stick and the rowdy who hits me over the head with a stick perform exactly the same empirical function. One may be legitimate and I may thank the policeman for his defense of law and order before I get to the hospital, and I might ask the policeman to arrest the rowdy who has hit me over the head. But in terms of what happens to my head, it is exactly the same thing. The same is true with killing in war.

War is organized violence. There is no empirical difference between the assassin who stabs me in the back and the soldier who impales the enemy on his bayonet. Morally sensitive philosophers have been fully aware of the physical identity of the action. Pascal said, If I kill you on this side of the river, I am an assassin; if I kill you on the other side of the river, I am a hero. Violence is a very delicate and politically, morally, and philosophically complex matter, much more ambiguous

---

11. The following nine paragraphs digress into a discussion of the role of violence in politics. This could be seen to follow from the last sentence of the previous paragraph concerning the relationship between political equality and the right to rule. It might also, however, have arisen from a student question. As noted in the introduction, the earlier editor of the text took out student questions from some earlier lectures, while leaving them in later lectures. My suspicion, although it is only a suspicion, is that this digression may have been prompted by a student question. Nevertheless, the following paragraphs do provide some interesting insights on how Morgenthau viewed the relationship between governance and the use of force, and so I have included them here.

than the present advocacy or opposition to violence would indicate. If you look at political history and ask yourself how the ultimate questions of political power have been settled, who should hold supreme political power, during most of history the question has been settled by violence. Look at the Old Testament. How was the succession to kingship decided? By who could kill whom. Look at the plays of Shakespeare—Richard II, Richard III, and so forth. How was the succession to the British throne decided? By who could kill whom. Look at Stalin, his succession to Lenin, and the succession to Stalin. Beria[12] is not going to compete for supreme political power in Russia anymore.

The democratic, civilized way of deciding the issue of who shall hold political power through the ballot box—and the defeated candidate leaving the White House and going back to Texas, or whatever state it may be—is a very delicate flower of a very high political civilization. It's an exception to the rule, and one ought not to forget that. We are not to forget how close violence has always been to the surface of political life. Our shock that is now emerging should not blind us to the fact that it has always been there. The absence of violence as the ultimate arbiter of political conflict is an exception to the violence rule.

Consider the Roman Empire. They killed each other off—their wives, their sisters, their mothers, everybody, in order to get supreme power and stay there. This went on for a couple of centuries. The same is true in the Orient. Take a look at the history of Thailand, for example. It's absolutely fantastic, the killing going on at the top. There was a king at the beginning of the nineteenth century who on the death of his father killed, I think, in one night 83 members of the royal family to make sure there was no competition. Take the history of the Indian kings. The history of Rajasthan, which a British colonel wrote, describes poisoning and the killing as an instrument of political conflict that is absolutely staggering.[13] The same is true if you look at the history of the popes. In the sixteenth century there was a papal coronation dinner to which the cardinals brought their own cooks because they wanted to come out alive. Machiavelli simply looked at the political world as it is, and Plato and Aristotle looked at it as it ought to be, according to a particular conservative interest. Aristotle, of course, was much more realistic than Plato. In Aristotle you find an enormous number of empirically and eternally valid observations.

Violence, then, is the last word in certain periods of history and in extreme circumstances. But after all, killing is not going to go on continuously and not on a large scale. The king who has come to power in civil war by killing his competitor has to rule, and he has to be careful that he is not killed. While he preserves his life, he must rule; and he must rule in a certain fashion. Especially in modern

---

12. Lavrenti Pavlovich Beria (1899–1953) served in the Soviet Union's secret police, eventually becoming its leader. He was executed in 1953 on conspiracy charges.

13. I believe Morgenthau refers here to the following history: James Tod, *Annals and Antiquities of Rajast'han, or the Central and Western Rajpoot States of India* (London: Smith Elder and Co., 1829–1832).

democracies you can rule only with the consent of the people. You need moral instruments of persuasion and certain moral restraints beyond which the rule would become intolerable to the people. Then there was the ever-present threat of revolution.

Today against the modern state like the government of the United States, a revolution is impossible. Talk about revolution is an illusion. Before the modern technologically advanced state—before the Bolshevik Revolution of 1917—all governments were aware, sometimes instinctively, of the fact that if they would overstep a certain line, they would face the wrath of the people, the violence from below. In order to guard against violence from below they had to rule within certain limits effectively without too obvious arbitrariness. For this kind of rule you need principles, and political philosophy supplies those principles, as Aristotle does when he develops different types of government.

Even the modern industrial state, however, cannot really completely do what it wants because it must then assure the loyalty of its bureaucracy, and more particularly, of its armed forces, which are also part of the people, a particular segment of the people, and partake in the moral and political preference of the people. In a modern state the military becomes infinitely more important under crisis conditions than the people at large. When France was threatened with revolution in May 1969, de Gaulle did not appeal to the people. He went to Baden-Baden, the headquarters of the French army in Germany, to General Massu, and got his support. In return he released the military prisoners who had been convicted of sedition and other crimes during the Algerian crisis. De Gaulle could not have governed without the army.[14]

In a less dramatic form, you find this situation in our government. I have been told time and time again that a certain policy cannot be pursued, even though it is recognized that it would be desirable, because the president cannot allow himself to buck the joint chiefs of staff. You find time and again that the civilian government is convinced that a certain policy is wrong, but the Joint Chiefs of Staff want it, so a compromise is concluded. Take ABM [Antiballistic Missile (System)].[15] The Joint Chiefs of Staff want to cover the whole country with an ABM system, which costs $50 billion perhaps and is completely useless. The administration says that we are going to establish a *thin* ABM system against China, which is absolute nonsense. Then we are going to develop first two ABM's around missile sites in one town in Wyoming, and then we are going to have four more. In other

---

14. General Jacques Massu (1908–2002) was a French military commander involved in many of France's conflicts during the mid-twentieth century. He is most well known for his service in Algeria, where he used controversial methods to suppress the Algerian resistance. The story to which Morgenthau is referring is open to interpretation. While de Gaulle did go to Baden-Baden during the 1969 riots, there are numerous conflicting reports about the purpose of the visit and what transpired between the two men. The example might, although it does not necessarily, prove Morgenthau's point. I am indebted to John Panktratz and Guilluame de Syon of Albright College for information on Massu.

15. This was an ongoing debate in disarmament talks during the late 1960s and early 1970s.

words, a child says I want to have the whole pudding and we tell him we will give you four raisins, which ought to satisfy you for the time being. This is much more important in terms of American government than the separation of powers or whatever constitutional doctrine you can think of. For this reason those factors are not generally discussed in classes in political science.

A system based on force is inherently unstable, like Aristotle's description of a tyrant. Therefore, the need for political conventions and philosophy persist. Somebody said that after the Revolution of 1848 in Prussia that you can do anything with bayonets, except sit on them. Certainly with brute force, especially with the kind of force that a modern government possesses, you can do a great deal: You can fill the prisons, you can deport people, you can shoot people. But you cannot really effectively govern them. In order to govern effectively, you have to have the consent of the people. If the taxi drivers in New York do not consent to the economic policies of the rulers, they will go on strike Monday and will paralyze the transportation system of New York. If the subway workers withhold their consent, they will go on strike as they did a couple of years ago. A government is an infinitely complex enterprise. By force you can rise to supreme power, but by force alone you cannot govern. Force remains, as the medieval writers said, the ultimate resort of kings. The term "ultimate" implies that in the day-by-day operations of government, you need certain principles, certain devices, procedures, and institutions. This is what political science or political philosophy deals with.

I said that the justification of slavery is that it serves the interest of the slave.[16] You have here in section 1255 a beautiful statement by Aristotle: "Where the relation of master and slave between them is natural they are friends and have a common interest, but where it rests merely on law and force the reverse is true."[17] In other words, the difference between legal and natural slavery is again emphasized. Also, they are friends and the relationship is beneficial as long as the master exercises his authority and lordship, which nature intended him to have. The abuse of this authority is injurious to both—the part and the whole, the body and soul are the same and the slave is a part of the master, a living but separated part of his bodily frame. Here you have again this assumption of a natural harmony of interests that completely overlooks the fact of power, which is always experienced by the object of power as an abuse.

What does political power really mean? That A uses B for his purposes. A imposes his will upon the will of B. This is what Aristotle calls the master-slave relationship. This imposition of the will of A on the will of B is always experienced by B (if he is not completely befogged by ideologies) as an infringement upon his freedom. That the ruled may have an aspiration for freedom is completely neglected by Aristotle. This problem has arisen very clearly in the Soviet Union. You

---

16. Morgenthau now returns to the line of argument that he had been pursuing prior to the digression concerning violence.

17. Aristotle, *The Politics* 1255b10-15.

have a regime that, like the master in Aristotle, maintains that it has the qualities to rule, morally, intellectually, that it is the legitimate successor to Marx and Lenin, executed in the truth inherent in the writings of Marx and Lenin; and the rest of the population, the ruled, the great masses of people, must obey those who by nature have been selected to rule. The population, however, does not accept this rule; large segments of the population do not accept that rule as natural. They regard it as an imposition and as an infringement upon their freedom and revolt in however limited a way against it. In other words, the organic conception of the state leads to the permanent subordination of the ruled to the will of the rulers. The assumption that the will of the rulers is in accordance with nature is, according to Aristotle himself, of very limited value. He says that the abuse of this authority is possible, that it is injurious to both. But he says nothing at all about what to do if that authority is abused or what to do if it is in the nature of that authority to be abused. The very exercise of that authority in a sense is experienced by the ruled as an abuse. This is the essential ambivalence of the political relationship. However beneficial the rule is intended to be, it is experienced by the ruled as an infringement upon their freedom. They may not be conscious of this. This is a Marxist conception of consciousness. The people may not be conscious of it, but once they are conscious of it, they revolt against it.

The organic concept of the state is not supported by Marxist political philosophy, which is rather a return to a state of nature. Here lies the similarity between the organic doctrine of the state and the return to nature that you have in Rousseau, Marx, and contemporary subcultures, such as youth cultures. This is not organic because it is not based upon a fixed division of labor after the model of the human body. Marx argued that the state in which man finds himself—alienation from the fruits of his labor, alienation from himself—is against nature. The fullness of human existence has to be restored through the classless society, the class division of society being the source of this alienation. But this is not organic in the sense in which the term is used as a technical term to characterize a particular type of political philosophy. This is a typical Rousseauist conception of a good state of nature, which once existed and which has been corrupted by a particular kind of society or, in the sense of Rousseau, by society as such.

What is the argument that one can make against this doctrine, particularly against its Marxist version? Against Rousseau's statement that man is born free and everywhere else he is in chains, the argument has been made that the statement is nonsensical because you don't have an empirical state of nature in which man was actually free. The Marxist version is exposed to the argument that the corruption of society, the exploitation of man by man, the alienation of man, are not the results of the class division of society but of human nature itself of which the class division of society is also a manifestation. In other words, the evil is in man himself, his lust for power, which leads to the class division of society. As we have seen, we have a self-proclaimed classless society in the Soviet Union; but certainly the exploitation of man by man, the arbitrary rule, a strict distinction between the rulers and the ruled has not been eliminated because it is inherent in human nature. If it is inherent in human nature then you have to create institutions, moral principles, moral and political restraints, checks and balances that are likely to restrain those exploitive and power hungry aspirations that are inherent in human nature. This is really the philosophy of the American Constitution, because it is extremely pessimistic about human nature. If you read the Federalist Papers you will see on every page how afraid the Founding Fathers were of the power tendencies of human nature. I think it was Lord Bryce who said that the American Constitution and political system are inspired by the theology of Calvin and the philosophy of Hobbes.[18] They have a profound pessimistic conception of human nature.

This, in fact, is the difference between the optimists and the pessimists, the liberals and the traditionalists. One says the evils that we see are the result of society. Change society and through it human nature, and you have solved the problem. The other says that the evils of society are the results of a human nature that is essentially unchangeable. Therefore you have to create moral and political and social contrivances that hem human nature in, which put artificial restraints upon it, which allow it only to do so much and not more. In our society we find that economic competition, economic exploitation has taken the place in the political struggle of violence. Mr. Rockefeller did not go out to kill Mr. Goldberg, which he would have done 300 years ago. He used his money and particular weaknesses of Mr. Goldberg to win the election. Even if Mr. Goldberg had been less weak as a candidate than he was, the enormous amount of economic power that Rockefeller could put into the balance might have decided the issue.[19]

Of course there are limits to the power of money. You cannot buy the whole Republican Convention. But it is certainly true that the amount of money you can spend on a campaign has enormous influence—not always, but frequently the decisive influence—something that has now become a matter of public debate and even of legislation by Congress, vetoed by the president [Nixon]. In former periods of history you would not have gone around hat in hand to the oil companies or to the public utilities to get money. You would have organized a private army and you would have won the political contest like that. There is no doubt that the economic influence upon political contests is undesirable, but it is still more desirable than going out and killing your opponent.

Returning again to the question of slavery in Chapter 13 of Book 1 it is very interesting how civilized Aristotle is within the general context of the defense of slavery. I should say again, what Aristotle has to say about slavery is really for us the argument in favor of political inequality. We have to abstract from slavery and ask ourselves what are the possible arguments in favor of political inequality in contrast to the democratic assumption of political equality. It is obvious how exaggerated this concept of democratic political equality is. How long has it been

---

18. Viscount James Bryce (1838–1922), a British scholar and statesman.
19. Morgenthau refers here to the 1970 New York gubernatorial race between Nelson Rockefeller (Republican) and Arthur Goldberg (Democrat).

since women have received the franchise? Not even fifty years in the United States. Until fifty years ago it was generally held, as a matter of course, that women were exactly in the position that Aristotle assigns to them, not capable of rational judgment that would entitle them to active participation in political life. We take it for granted today, but you ought to read the history of the suffragettes and see how those women operated in order to get the franchise—hitting policemen, going to jail. Women's lib today is a parlor affair in comparison to what those women did, for the simple reason that there is very little from which women need to be liberated today. Fifty years ago they were liberated from the basic handicap that they were regarded as inferior political beings and inferior in general. The Aristotelian conception of the family and of the natural superiority of the man, the teleological predestination of the woman—kitchen, church, children (not necessarily in that sequence)—and the teleological monopoly of the male as the rational leader, not only in politics but in all affairs, has been abolished very recently. In other words, fifty years ago we were much closer to Aristotle than we were to the modern conception of the equality of men and women.

The question I am really raising here is the enormously civilized way in which Aristotle maintains the distinction between slave and master. He says here, "A question may indeed be raised whether there is any excellence at all in a slave beyond entire and higher than merely instrumental and ministerial qualities. Whether he can have the virtues of temperance, courage, justice and the like or whether slaves possess only bodily and ministerial qualities and whichever way we answer the question a difficulty arises, for if they have virtue in what will they differ from freemen." How do you maintain the distinction between rulers and ruled if you assign virtue to the slaves? On the other hand, since they are men in body and rational principle, it seems absurd to say that they have no virtue. I am also reading this in order to show the much greater moral sophistication of Aristotle as over contemporary or modern defenders of slavery and racial inequality. "A similar question may be raised about women and children—whether they too have virtues or ought a woman be temperate and brave and just. And is a child to be called temperate and intemperate or not. So in general we may ask about the natural ruler and the natural subject whether they have the same or different virtues; for if a noble nature is equally required in both, why both, why should one of them always rule and the other always be ruled."

This is very profound and in a sense very just. Only the answer is unjust, but the question he raises is enormously sensitive in moral terms. "Nor can we say that this is a question of degree for the difference between rule and subject is a difference of kind which the difference of more or less never is. Yet how strange is the supposition that the one ought and the other ought not to have virtue. For if the ruler is intemperate and unjust how can he rule well? If the subject, how can he obey well? If he is licentious and cowardly he will certainly not do his duty. It is evident therefore that both of them must have a share of virtue but varying as natural subjects also vary amongst themselves." This is a classic example of Aristotelian argument, which shows how great a thinker Aristotle was.

He connects the virtues of the different classes of people with their telos. "Moral virtues belong to all of them, but the temperance of a man and of a woman or the courage of a man and of a woman are not the same. The courage of a man is shown in commanding, of a woman in obeying. . . ." and so forth. His virtue is not relative to himself alone but to the perfect man.

Then again the justification of political inequality in terms of the interests of the ruled—which is again a very typical conservative and even totalitarian argument—that is, the Politburo is the source of all virtue and wisdom because it is the authentic successor of Marx and Lenin. Anyone who denies this or expresses a different opinion is a usurper, a wrecker, a heretic. "It is manifest then that the master ought to be the source of such excellence in the slave and not a mere possessor of the art of mastership which trains the slave in his duties." In other words, the master should not be an exploiter of a slave, ruling over him for his own sake, but for the sake of the slave himself. "Wherefore they are mistaken who forbid us to converse with slaves and say that we should employ command only, for slaves stand even more in need of admonition than children."

We will discuss today the problem of equality as it is discussed in Chapter 12 of the third book of Aristotle's *The Politics*.[20] As you well remember, Aristotle says, "The state is created not only for the preservation of life," in the sense in which Hobbes speaks of the creation of the state, "but for the sake of the good life." And so, the basic problem is, what is the difference between life per se and the good life? The good life is a life that is led by justice, which is also, of course, indicated by the general conception of politics that was dominant both in the Middle Ages and in antiquity, that the philosophy of politics is really a subdivision of ethics. I am not identifying myself with this. I am just reporting what the basic outlook at that time was. And so, inevitably Aristotle is led to what he regards to be in his system of philosophy the central issue, that is, the issue of justice. "In all sciences and arts the end is the good, and the greatest good and in the highest degree and the most authoritative of all this is the political science of which the good is justice, in other words, the common interest." We have already talked about the common interest and I shall not go into this here again.[21] Let's skip this identification of justice with the common interest that is a very dubious one. But let's go to the next statement, which is crucial: "All men think justice to be a sort of equality." This is, of course, obvious. You have only to consider today in our

20. Here begins a seminar that Morgenthau conducted on January 8, 1971. As he states, he is now addressing a chapter in Book 3 of *The Politics*, Chapter 12, in which Aristotle explores the question of equality. While Morgenthau had chosen to examine the question of equality in his discussion of Book 1, where Aristotle discusses the differences among men, women, and slaves, Aristotle does not address equality in that passage. In other words, Book 3, Chapter 12 of *The Politics* is the first place Aristotle explicitly turns to equality. I have chosen to move this section from its sequential order in the lecture series to this position because it further reinforces some of the themes Morgenthau explored in his discussion of Book 1. I have tried to eliminate repetitive sections.

21. See Chapter 5, "Power, Interests, and the Common Good."

society the issues of justice with regard to migratory workers, slum dwellers, or the justice to certain ethnic minorities, such as blacks, Puerto Ricans, and Mexican Americans. What is the basic issue? The basic issue is the issue of equality. In other words, when we talk about justice, we are really talking about equality. And what we find unjust about the treatment of all the groups I have just mentioned is that they are not dealt with equally. When we speak of discrimination, what we are really saying is that the treatment of all people is not equal. The housing that is available to the white American is not available to the black American. Or that hiring practices are discriminatory because people are not hired on the basis of equality, but race is made a distinctive characteristic that works as a handicap for certain ethnic groups.

Aristotle also argues that all differences among men ought to be disregarded altogether and that some kind of abstract equality ought to reign regardless of any differences whatsoever. This is not the issue, because this is an absurd proposition. The real proposition is that people ought to be—and this is what justice requires—that people ought to be dealt with on an equal footing with regard to those qualities that are relevant for a particular decision. If you assume that there are genetic differences between individuals that are relevant, let me say, for hiring practices, if you assume that blacks or Chicanos or Puerto Ricans are naturally lazy, unintelligent, sloppy, or any other characteristics on which racial discrimination is based, of course the discriminators have a point. Because if it is true that certain races are genetically given to lower performances or are untrustworthy, dishonest by nature, obviously you are not going to hire them as bank tellers, policemen, or for any job in which honesty, reliability, precision, and so forth are required and necessary. So the issue of equality is still the central issue of justice. And the real problem is, and the problem that has baffled both the philosophers and practitioners throughout history is, what are the relevant criteria? In what respect is it justified to discriminate? In what respect is it not? For instance, if I were to enter the race for the world championship in boxing, obviously I would be rejected out of health. People would take one look at me and they'd say, "My God, go away." And I would say, "You are discriminating against me. You are anti-Semitic, perhaps, or what not." But obviously here is a discrimination that is perfectly justified, because in terms of the standards that are applicable, that are to determine participation in the world championship for boxing, obviously all of us here are to a greater or lesser extent excluded because we don't measure up to the standards necessary for participating in the world championship for boxing. But let's suppose somebody would say to me, "The color of your hair—" or, let me put it crudely, somebody would say, "White men are not allowed to participate in the championship for boxing. Only black men are." That would be evidently a discriminatory exclusion, because the color of one's skin is obviously not a valid criterion for distinguishing between those who are allowed and those who are not allowed to participate in the world championship for boxing. In this case it is simple. But in other cases it is enormously difficult.

Consider the problem of discrimination between the sexes. Certainly, well, I shouldn't say certainly because up to the 1920s throughout history it was assumed that women genetically were not capable of arriving at sound political judgments, and for this reason they were excluded from the ballot. In any event, for millennia it was taken for granted that the unequal treatment of men and women with regard to political rights was not unjust because it was based upon a natural difference that was relevant for the exercise of political rights. We don't believe that any more, and so if women were today to be excluded from political activity and also from running for certain elective offices, we would regard this as clearly discriminatory. So the problem of justice and the way we conceive of the problem of justice and put it into practice is intimately connected, is organically connected, with our empirical conception as to what the differences among different groups are and what the relevance of those differences is for the exercise of political rights.

Consider again the problem of women. If you assume that women are essentially emotional and men are essentially rational, that rational, dispassionate objective judgment is a prerequisite of the exercise of political rights, you are perfectly justified in excluding women from the exercise of political rights. But if still you assume that rational judgment is required for the exercise of political rights, and then you assume that this rational judgment is not the monopoly of one sex or that the absence of it, which is probably a more correct statement from an empirical point of view, is distributed in both sexes in a matter of degree rather than of kind, so that you have a lot of judgments of a nonrational character among male policymakers, and if you look at the analysis of election results, of course you realize, through the voting patterns, that that empirical distinction is simply not valid. So then you arrive at the conclusion that the distinction on the basis of sex is untenable on empirical grounds, and that then discrimination on that basis would be unjust, would be discriminatory.

The deprivation of women of political rights was, of course, not based upon empirical evidence of any validity, but was based upon empirical evidence that was the result of cultural conditioning. You put women into the kitchen—well, you know the three functions of women: A woman should bear children, should cook, and should go to church. So once you have created this kind of cultural situation and leave it to the men to take care of politics, your arrangement became a self-fulfilling prophecy. We could afterwards point to the actual functions women perform as proof of your preconception. We have a very similar situation, for instance, with a conception that was very common in Europe: that Jews were congenitally incapable of military and agricultural activity; that Jews were by nature genetically driven to commerce, banking, money-lending, and so forth. Culturally, empirically speaking, this was true, but it was the result of certain arrangements that excluded Jews from owning land or from entering the military service. And so it is with women. In other words, you have here a cultural arrangement that supports your philosophic conception, your discriminatory conception, and appears to give empirical evidence to it. And we don't realize that it has been created, that the empirical evidence has been artificially created by the cultural arrangement.

Another way to consider this same issue of equality is to think about political judgment. Most of the people I know who deal with foreign policy are devoid of political judgment. It is a very rare quality. So I would not exclude a priori the proposition that people are different by nature in different respects, and that they are also different with regard to politics. And if one could find a yardstick by which one could separate the black and the white sheep, if it were as simple as that, I would be in favor of it. I'm convinced that only a small minority is capable of governing. Most of the people who govern are unqualified to govern. And we don't have to go back into ancient history to notice that. It is only by sheer accident that somebody comes up who is capable of governing. I wouldn't know what the test is, but I think the difference is obvious. If you had made a test in terms of culture, Truman would certainly have flunked in terms of education, general outlook. Moreover, he owed his political career to one of the foulest political machines ever created in the country, the Kansas City Machine. Take Lincoln. Lincoln was a kind of country bumpkin. A slightly funny fellow, the caricatures of the time show it. When he was a lawyer for the Union Pacific, he represented the Union Pacific in a lawsuit in St. Louis. And the New York lawyers who also were called for by the Union Pacific refused to sit beside him because he looked so disreputable. Yet he was certainly the greatest American president, and in certain respects probably a uniquely great statesman by any standards.

So you have a problem, which, in my view at least, cannot be solved by rational methods. I think it is true, and experience shows it, that there is an enormous difference among people with regard to the qualities that go into statesmanship, that go into the making of good politics. I think this is something one can take for granted. And the issue that cannot be resolved, at least in my view, by rational means is: How do you devise a test that at least maximizes the chances that the people capable or endowed with those qualities that go into the making of good politics rise to the top and not the others? This is the real issue. In other words, how do you deal with equals on an equal basis with regard to those qualities that are essential for making good policy? This is the crucial issue of any constitution.

There are two extremes. One is the great leader who combines within himself those qualities that go into the making of statesmanship, good political leadership, and so forth; and he is, of course, not elected generally by any standards that are relevant to his qualities, like in the case of Lincoln. By a mere accident of history he rises to the top, while, if the historic configuration would have been different, he would never have risen to the top and nobody would ever have heard of him. And probably you can take it for granted that there are a number of Lincolns or a number of great statesmen who never were able to show that they were great statesmen because they never had the political power to show it. Aristotle says those people are really above politics and nothing one can say philosophically of politics applies to them. They are really like gods among men. Take a man like Napoleon with regard to whose leadership, of course, you can be of quite different opinions. You can say that he was a very great leader—a genius, a political and more particularly a military genius—and therefore it was right that he should come to the top. But there are lots of people who say that Napoleon was an un-mitigated disaster for France and for Europe. He bled France white, and if you look at the result in 1815, it was for nothing. France was reduced to its historic frontiers, the Rhine frontier, and so forth. And all the conquests of Napoleon were lost at an enormous price of human life, human happiness, material welfare, and so forth.

In any case, there is a difference between the national interest of France and the personal interests of Napoleon. You see, it is still then an open question if there rises a man with those superhuman capacities for political and military leader-ship, should he be selected, if he is to be found by any objective standard, to lead a nation, or should he be allowed to lead a nation if he rises through the struggle for power to the top? His rule may well be a disaster for the nation. And here Aris-totle discusses the problem of ostracism as an institution. In other words, you send the most powerful man away either for a time or for life because the political com-monwealth cannot support such enormous power. Which comes back to the prob-lem of equality. First you select, or you allow a man to rise to the top because he has in abundance those qualities that go into the making of political leadership. Then you create, of course, extreme inequality because here is that one man, all powerful, and here is the mass of the citizens who are to a greater or lesser extent subject to his power. So if you are interested in equality as a political status, or a political relationship, you cannot tolerate people or organizations who are so powerful that their power and the power of the rest of the citizens are extremely disparate and political equality is thereby really destroyed.

How to preserve political equality after one has established it is the second problem to which the issue of equality gives rise. If you let nature take its course, if you say, for instance, as I have just said, there are certain qualities that go into the making of political leadership and good politics—and let me suppose you have discovered them and the man who meets those standards has come to the top—you are right away faced with a second problem, and that is that you have created one man or a small group of men who are politically superior to the oth-ers to such a degree that they destroy political society. So that the great mass of citizens become the subjects of the political leaders and political equality is sim-ply abolished. And the question, of course, arises, what do you do about that? As I have said, as Aristotle points out, the Greeks had an institution—ostracism—for the purpose of periodically recreating political equality by removing those indi-viduals who had become too powerful for political equality. But is this a reliable method of restoring political equality? This leads to the absolute denial of equal-ity. And if you identify justice and equality, you have the epitome of injustice be-cause the great majority of the people are deprived of their political rights or at least are incapable of exercising them because of the extreme discrepancy in po-litical power.

Aristotle gets out of this by a trick. He says those charismatic leaders are like gods and the rule of politics do not apply to them. But of course they apply to them because the basic issues of political justice are magnified by the rise of such a godlike charismatic leader. One of the requirements of political equality is that the power of the government is limited, which Aristotle calls constitutional government. Even the most powerful can only go so far and not farther before he is checked by some kind of institutional arrangement, in the American constitution by the system of checks and balances, that one branch of the government is supposed to check the other branches in order to prevent any one of them from accumulating unchallengeable power and, thereby, destroying political equality. But where you have a charismatic leader, this remedy is not available because by the very definition of charismatic leadership, as Aristotle has put it, this leader is above the laws, is a kind of a god who is not subject to those limitations. But then, since he is only like a god and not a god himself, he is subject to the same corruptive influences of power as the rest, only to a much greater extent because his power is much greater. And this is, of course, obvious if you look at the history of charismatic leadership. A man like Napoleon, a man like Bismarck, to give only two examples—it is obvious in them that the enormous power also led to enormous corruption. In other words, even the most powerful human is not virtuous and wise enough to limit himself in the exercise of his power. And so the issue of political equality is not transcended by the emergence of a charismatic leader. It is only confirmed, confirmed with much greater intensity than when we deal with ordinary people, the average politician. In other words, you have to deal in politics with a number of insoluble antinomies that are simply the result of the existential inequality inherent in politics, which is the fact that one man rules over another man, exercises power over another man, imposes his will upon the will of another man, which is, of course, the paradigm of inequality.

And this is the culminating paradox—that a just political order is based upon the principle of equality, but it is in the very nature of politics that it divides men on the basis of inequality. Of course, you can, and in our society we have seen this, you can put the principle of equality above everything else and you are then logically driven toward copping out of politics. You may say, symbolically, the Woodstock culture is the denial of politics itself because it puts freedom over everything else. And that brings me to the issue of freedom. Political equality in its strict sense is identical with political freedom because you are only completely free if you have nobody who lords above you. In other words, equality and freedom are identical. What does political equality mean? It means I'm free from the rule of somebody else.

This raises the point of political order and its relationship to freedom. Political order is an infringement on freedom. You may also say that whatever freedom you have got is predicated upon political order. But that doesn't deny the first proposition. In other words, you have here a number of antinomies that are, in my view, logically insoluble. There can only be an accommodation and a modus vivendi, some kind of compromise, if you want to call it that. But one has to be clear in one's own mind that the antinomy exists. Consider the example of Robert

Owen,[22] who wanted to escape, who wanted to have political freedom in completeness and went to America and created the communes and so forth. Logically, this is the only way in which you can establish complete equality and complete freedom, because a policeman who stops me on the street also is an expression of inequality. He can stop me, but I can't stop him. You might have experienced this, as I have, that you rationally recognize the right of the policeman and the necessity of the policeman's functions. Still there is a temporary hurt in that part of your psychological constitution where the desire for equality rests, however slight a traumatic experience. You hate to be stopped by another guy who happens to run around in a uniform with a stick and a revolver. This denial of your equality that is identical with the denial of your freedom is existential. Let me say, you have here individuals. They are equal and they are free. If there is inequality—this man is superior to this man—it means also an infringement upon his freedom, because political inequality is identical with impairment of political freedom. And complete freedom can only exist among complete equals.

My point here is not an anarchist one. I'm fully aware of the inevitability of inequality. I only want to show what the structure of political life is without expressing any preferences or arguing for or against anything. What I'm saying is that anarchism has a valid point in theory when it says, you want to be free, you Democrats or you Liberals! You say you value freedom, but look at the kind of society in which you live where the policeman can stop you, where the tax collector can take your money away, where the draft board can put you into uniform and send you to your death; you are not free. And they're right in this argument, as far as it goes. Of course, this absolute freedom, identical with absolute equality, does not work in practice, as the history of communes and the history of anarchic societies has shown. Because those anarchistic societies or those societies like the Owen Society, which are based upon absolute equality, transform themselves into hierarchical structures. And that is the next question we have to raise: Why is that so?

The point I am making is that in this particular respect—and this is true of any other situation where one man can impose his will upon another by the exercise of political power—there exists "unfreedom" with regard to this particular situation. There exists inequality. In other words, there exists an organic relationship among political power, political freedom, and political equality. And they are all, you may say, aspects of the same relationship. Here is A—let me say the tax collector or the draft official or the policeman—in some respect having power over B. By the same token that A has power over B, in the same measure the freedom of B is abrogated by the power of A. Furthermore, this power relationship of A and B also implies a relationship of inequality.

At the same time, the very biological needs of the perpetuation of the race require a certain inequality and a certain authority. Whether the mother or the father or the family as a whole is exerting it, this is beside the point; but somebody has

---

22. Robert Owen (1771–1858), the British utopian socialist who moved to America to create the community of New Harmony in Indiana.

to keep order in the family. And so this picture is, of course, a Hobbesian abstraction which in actuality doesn't exist because nobody, no human being, no animal as a matter of fact, comes into the world as an independent, free, and equal being. By the very fact that he comes into the world as a helpless infant, he is subject to the authority of others. He is biologically unequal. There comes a point in the biological development where authoritative assistance of others is no longer needed. This is certainly correct. And this is what you have in animal societies very clearly, that once biologically the individual is capable of surviving, it becomes independent.

But the real reason why inequality is inevitable, political or otherwise, and where the exercise of power and the concomitant limitation on freedom are also inevitable, is first of all the result of, you may say, the natural wickedness of individuals who simply will not spontaneously obey the rules that are required for the survival of society. As the *Federalist Papers* say, if men were angels, you wouldn't need a government. It is exactly because they are not angels, that they don't spontaneously comply with the rules necessary for society, that you need what the Manchester liberals call the Night Watchman State to keep a certain modicum of order in society. The second reason why you, at least empirically, haven't had complete equality, complete freedom and absence of power, is that the interests of individuals and the disparate aspirations of individuals, and consequently their different abilities, create natural cleavages in society, natural inequalities that transform themselves into political power and lack of political freedom. Let's take the example of nineteenth-century liberalism, which thought that the only threat to freedom, the only source of political inequality was the existence of government, especially of strong government. The more you restrict the powers of government, the greater will be individual freedom and individual equality.

But what happened? You had a government, a laissez-faire government, a night watchman conception of government, and out of the autonomous interplay of social forces extreme inequalities of economic power, social power, political power arose. Again with the concept of loss of freedom of large masses of individuals. And where is the source of those inequalities? In the different interests of individuals, different aspirations of individuals, and more particularly in the differential in the abilities of those individuals to satisfy their aspirations.

Lots of people wanted to dominate the oil interests of the United States, and they competed with each other, and one, the founder of the Rockefeller dynasty, succeeded. And he drove thousands of independent oil dealers and producers into bankruptcy and suicide. But he succeeded. And all of a sudden you had a center of political, economic, and social power that was the result of the free competition among what you might call "naturally unequals." The robber barons in general are examples of this kind. And so you got enormous concentrations of unregulated social, political, and economic power that the government watched without interfering. Thus, the laissez-faire state brought about extreme inequalities. And the extremity of those inequalities forced the state to intervene on behalf of the disadvantaged by regulating, controlling, trying to dissolve the concentrations of private power. In other words, what you got was a kind of feudalism in which the autonomous social forces created centers of private power, which in many respects became more powerful than the centers of public power. And you have today a situation in which certain concentrations of private power in the form of giant corporations or labor unions are much more capable of governing than the public authorities—a situation in which the public authorities have to negotiate as one sovereign with another sovereign in order to keep society going, at least within certain limits.

If you look at the structure of medieval feudalism, where the king had to negotiate and bargain with the feudal lords, giving up certain of his powers in order to get the support he needed from them, you realize how similar the relations between private and public governments today are to the classic feudalism. It would be an excellent doctoral thesis for somebody to develop this analogy. Of course, generally those subjects are not preferred for obvious political reasons, again for reasons of political inequality and what not. I haven't the time to do it, but I find it a fascinating topic to see how the medieval government worked, where the king had to beg the feudal lords to support him or to pursue policies that were favorable to him, much as the federal government must beg the steel companies not to raise their prices, and the unions to use self-restraint in their wage demands, without being able to do anything about it.

You can say that the American economy is at the mercy of certain gigantic concentrations of private power that are really private governments, feudal governments, and the fate of the nation to a great extent depends not upon what the public government does, but what these private governments do. In order to keep a modicum of order and to keep society together, public authorities have to bargain and negotiate with the private governments. In order to have protection against fires, the government of New York cannot give orders; it has to bargain with the organization of the firefighters like one sovereign power with the other. So this is, of course, the ultimate source of political inequality, which lies in human nature, in the different aspirations, and more particularly the abilities to satisfy those aspirations among different individuals and groups of individuals. So there is no escape from those natural inequalities, neither in the form of anarchy nor in the form of a so-called classless society.

Indeed, as we see in the Soviet Union and in other socialist or communist countries, the old classes have been destroyed. They are no longer capitalists and proletarians in the classic sense, but new classes have risen, new distinctions, new political inequalities have been created that are the result again of the different aspirations and different abilities of different people.

This problem was raised at the Party Congress of 1939 when people raised the question, now that all the class enemies have been destroyed, why do we need a state? Why doesn't the state wither away? And Stalin got up and said, as politicians everywhere say, "That's a very good question. I am glad you asked that question." Stalin said, "Sure, we don't need the state for domestic purposes. We have a classless society. The class enemies have been destroyed. But we need a strong state because of the foreign enemies. Once all nations have gone Communist, we don't need a state any more." That was before China became Communist. "We don't need a state any more, but as long as we are faced with the capitalistic encirclement, we need one." And of course the truth is, as it is obvious today and has always been obvious throughout history, armed forces are needed first of all for domestic not for foreign political reasons. Because the army in most countries, as the police in most countries, is the backbone of the government. And most governments rule not by the will of the people but by the will of the army.

In this country this is still concealed because of the traditional political and constitutional arrangement, that is, by the traditional ethos that mistrusts the army. But there isn't any doubt that, if the chips are down in this country, what will decide is where the armed forces stand. Of course, one saving grace in this country is that the army is not a professional army but a drafted army, and most draftees hate the army.[23] So you haven't got an esprit de corps that go through the motions and do what they have to do because the disadvantages if they don't do it are too painful. But if a general would give orders tomorrow for the army to march on Washington, the army would string the general at the next lamppost. I said this the other day at the General Staff School at Leavenworth. The reaction was rather negative. I think they thought it was not a nice way of talking about people who are preparing to become generals themselves. But it is true. The American Army as presently constituted cannot be an instrument for domestic political purposes because it is, in however a distorted way, a replica of American society. And there is no political cohesion today that an ambitious general, such as General MacArthur or any other general, could use for his purposes. But of course, if you have a volunteer army, you might well have an entirely different situation, which, in my view, is an enormous risk one takes if one creates a volunteer army, because then somebody who voluntarily joins the army has already made a decision with regard to where he stands. And then you can have a cohesive force that can be used for political purposes. And this is what the wisdom of the Founding Fathers and the *Federalist Papers* warned against.

How do we know this about human nature? In the abstract you can debate it, but in practice you all know that certain people have enormous power drives. Others have moderate power drives and others have very little, if any. Some people concentrate their power drives on making money, others on having as many different erotic experiences as possible. Don Juan is an example of such a power drive. Alexander in the political sphere is another one. We know that such people exist. We know that certain people have enormous power drives directed in one channel and others directed in another channel, and we have all those distinctions as facts. Human nature is simply shorthand for saying that those differences exist; whether they are genetic or socially acquired is a different question. But they certainly exist.

Here I part company with Marx. You see, for Marx what we call human nature was a product of society. But I would say, society is a product of human nature.

---

23. The U.S. Congress abolished the draft in 1973.

Marx starts with the assumption of the infinite malleability of human nature. The evil to which the flesh is heir is the result of a particular social arrangement. What we call original sin or the evil of man is the result of an evil society, the class society, which, wherever it came from, is there. Now I say, and the conclusion is obvious, get rid of that evil society and you have gotten rid of the evil in man. Then you will have a classless society where, as Marx and Engels put it at the end of the *Communist Manifesto*, the domination of men by men, the very fact of politics, inequality, the denial of freedom, will be replaced by the administration of things. But in my view, this is a Utopian prophecy because the great weakness of the Marxist conception of the relationship between society and man is that he starts with society as the original given, whereas in truth a particular man has created a particular society. It is not that you can change man and, especially, extirpate the evil in man by changing society. But you have to change man in order to change society, and this is a very hard thing to do. Herbert Marcuse theoretically is correct when he calls for a new man combining Freud and Marx.[24] He is correct, but how do you create a new man combining Freud and Marx? He is correct, but how do you create a new man short of the second coming of Christ or the coming of the Messiah? If you look at the Old Testament or Greek mythology, you see the same attributes in man that we see in him today. So I very strongly believe that this Marxist conception is a Utopian one, and that what you will do by creating a new society is shift the burden of inequality and unfreedom from one group of people to another one. But you are not going to eliminate it, and the experience that we have had with Communist and Socialist societies, I think, bears that analysis out.

---

24. Herbert Marcuse (1898–1979) was a German philosopher and social critic. A student of Martin Heidegger, he sought to reinvigorate the study of Marxism and was considered one of the leading philosophical defenders of the "New Left." Morgenthau is perhaps referring to *Eros and Civilization* (1955), in which Marcuse tried to combine Freud with Marxism.

CHAPTER 3

Law and Government

There are two problems I want to discuss in Book 3 before we go on to Book 4. One is Chapter 11 dealing with the problem of democracy in which Aristotle argues that of all the types of rule, perhaps the rule of the many, democracy, or the polity that is limited by the constitution is the best. Which is, if you look at the overall structure of Aristotelian thought, a surprising conclusion. And a conclusion that is completely at variance with the Platonic position. What argument does Aristotle use to justify the rule of the many as being superior to the rule of the few, or the rule of one man?

As far as qualification is concerned, obviously the aristocratic rule of the wealthy or the rule of the most qualified by training or by experience or by family or the rule of the expert ought to be a priori superior to the rule of the many. How does he argue here? He uses an argument that is not surprising under the circumstances. He argues that the many, when they meet together collectively, can surpass in quality the few. In other words, a nondescript member of the mass may be

This chapter derives from a number of different sources. The first section is from an undated manuscript included with the seminars in which Morgenthau explores *The Politics*, Book 3, Chapter 11 of Aristotle, a discussion of the benefits of the rule of the many. Following this section are two sets of student notes, both referring to the same seminar date (November 27, 1970). I have relied primarily on the notes taken by Martin Price, although I have borrowed a few passages from Anna Goldoff. Also, the following pages refer to a short section of *The Politics*, Book 2, 1268b5–1269a30, in which Aristotle discusses the dangers of changing the law even when it may be faulty. Aristotle's argument rests on his belief that "the law has no power to command obedience except that of habit, which can only be given by time, so that a readiness to change from old to new laws enfeebles the power of the law" (1269a20). Finally, included here is a selection from seminars conducted on March 1972 on the types of government. This chapter also introduces student questions for the first time, a change in format explained in more detail in the editor's introduction.

inferior to a judge of the Supreme Court but the people at large with their collective wisdom may be superior to a judge of a Supreme Court. He makes the comparison with the individual who may have certain faults and certain strong points, certain virtues, and if you look at him from a particular point of view with regard to a particularity, there is not much favorable to be said about him; but if you look at him as a whole, the whole is superior in quality to the sum total of its component parts, some of which may be inferior to others.

In other words, the collectivity has a particular virtue and a particular assumption of wisdom and general ability of qualification that the individual, or the mechanical sum of the individuals, does not have. Aristotle compares this political competence of the mass with aesthetic competence. Aristotle makes a point that the user of a thing may be superior in judgment to the creator; for example, the guy who lives in a house may know more about the requisite qualities of a house than the architect. If you transfer this technical argument to politics, the single individual may know what is needed by way of taxation and redistribution of wealth but he doesn't have the technical ability to do something about it. For this reason he elects the magistrates to do it for him. But then his judgment in the election of magistrates again reveals itself as superior, or possibly superior, to that of an individual who doesn't have this experience. There is here a division of labor: The judgment of the people at large can be trusted to identify the issues and to pass laws and, more particularly, to elect magistrates who are able to do something about it.

One might respond that because a certain expertise is necessary to appreciate a fine flute player and very few people can really understand fine flute playing, similarly in the government perhaps there are a few people that really understand what is going on politically. For Aristotle, however, the audience in an orchestra hall is capable of deciding what is a good or a bad performance, what is a good or a bad composition. The expert, let me say a famous critic, may be terribly biased or may be led astray by some kind of prejudice or vanity, while the good sense of the people at large can be trusted. You certainly have examples in the history of music when individual critics have damned new music, say in regard to Wagner, while the people at large have accepted the new music as valid. Or rather, I wouldn't say it was the people at large, I would say it was the people that knew something about Wagner, and they would be relatively few in number. Of course, this is another problem. When Aristotle talks about citizens, he talks about a very small group of highly qualified, highly educated people. He really talks about an aristocracy in our sense. When we talk about citizens in a democracy, we talk about millions of people. As you know, at the beginning of the book Aristotle points to the fact that only face to face relations can create a viable polity, a viable political unit. So we are dealing with extremely small entities. And you can imagine, so high a quality of judgment of so highly educated and sophisticated a group can be more trusted than the judgment of a single expert. I think this explains the confidence that Aristotle voices here in the people at large in an infinitely more narrow sense than we do. Because in itself if you apply this argument to our conception of citizenry, it seems to be extremely dubious; and it becomes even dubious in the argument of Aristotle later on when he puts the judgment of the citizen within the framework of the laws, because it is only within the laws that those judgments are valid. If there are no laws, as we shall see in a moment, the popular rule degenerates into autocracy.

What is the saving grace of a democracy? Obviously, and history is full of examples, a democratic rule can be outrageously deficient. Of course, so can the rule of a king or a tyrant. Certainly democracies can be deficient. But what is the saving grace of the mechanics of democracy—in counter-distinction to any other form of government? What is the difference between a bad totalitarian rule and a bad democratic rule? The difference is that there exists a possibility within the mechanics of democracy itself of a self-corrective. You can throw the scoundrels out! You can replace a deficient incompetent government with a decent one without interrupting the constitutional continuity within the dynamics and mechanics of the democratic process itself.

In other words, the democratic discussion itself, the marketplace of ideas, creates the possibilities for wise decisions and the correction of unwise ones. As for the ruler, his wisdom is perpetuated only in the rules, not in the person of the ruler. For this reason the rules are sacrosanct, while the ruler has to be elected according to conditions, circumstances, and judgment. The further question for Aristotle is whether or not being the best is a static or dynamic quality. The best ruler can become the worst ruler through the corruption of power or through the deficiencies of his judgment and his character.

Another danger is that the rulers are fully aware of the conditions of the people but that the vested interests—the people interested in the conservation of the status quo—are too powerful for the ruler to do anything about it. It is not a question of knowledge; it is a question of the distribution of power within society. The vested interests must curry the favor of the rulers because the rulers by definition have the power to benefit them or to damage them. The idea that Soviet Premier Khrushchev once expressed, that President Kennedy was receiving orders from the Rockefellers, is a little bit oversimplified. What you have and what you always have had is collusion between powerful economic interests and political powers; and insofar as the political powers have a need of financial support from the economic interests, the economic interests, of course, have a lever of power that will be used—it will buy certain favors. You are dealing here not with abstractions but with today's headlines.

The question that Aristotle at least raises, without dealing in great detail with it, is the relationship between a particular form of government and a social class. He says you may have a democratic constitution and an entirely non-democratic regime. Or you may have an aristocratic constitution and a democratic regime. In other words, the actuality of the distribution of power within the constitutional framework is decisive, and you can see this now in the failure of democratic constitutions superimposed upon anti-democratic social conditions in the Middle East or in Asia. In other words, a democratic reality in terms of social structure and moral values has to correspond to the democratic forms. And where it doesn't correspond, the social structure and the actual moral values will prevail over the democratic forms.

Student: Would it be meaningful to argue that, for instance, in Cuba you have a regime that is "tyrannical" or aristocratic, but that in content is democratic insofar as Castro is actually sensitive to carrying out the wishes of the majority of the Cuban population?

HJM: This is no criterion of the form of government. This could be true of a tyrant who is wise—wise enough to listen to the wishes of the people or of a king or of any ruler. But you raise another important point and that is, if you define democracy as government with the consent of the people, then certain totalitarianisms have indeed been democracies. Take Nazism. If you define democracy in terms of government by consent of the people, Hitler governed with the passionate and enthusiastic consent of the overwhelming majority of the people.

Student: Hitler was well aware of that, and repeatedly claimed the popular support he had was far ahead of that of any other democratic government. I think it was quite true.

HJM: Sure it was true. Even though it missed a very important point. But it was true as far as it went. What it missed was the ability of a genuine democratic regime to change rulers through constitutional processes. In other words, the Germans were stuck with Hitler for better or for worse. They couldn't remove him if they wanted to; they didn't want to, but they couldn't even if they wanted to. In a sense, that is true of Castro, too. The fundamental mistake of the Bay of Pigs was exactly not to understand this. The CIA thought that Castro was another Latin American dictator, superimposed upon an unwilling people who were waiting to get rid of him. In reality he was and is a plebiscitary dictator who has the overwhelming support of his people. So the consent of the people cannot be the decisive measure of democracy. And here again the wisdom of Aristotle reveals itself. He makes exactly this point. He says, "Mere majority rule is tyranny because it doesn't allow for any change in the ruler," for any organic process of change, as we would say, with regard to the rules that Aristotle doesn't recognize (for the reasons we have discussed before), with regard to the rulers, with regard to the election of magistrates. In other words, the consent of a dictatorship, even if it is spontaneous at the beginning, is maintained by totalitarian means and this is the essence of totalitarianism. You don't have the competition of different groups all having an equal chance for becoming the majority and being the rulers tomorrow. The ruler of today has a monopoly of political power, and he perpetuates the consent of the governed with totalitarian means—of terror, of propaganda, of the monopoly of the mass media, of education, and so forth.

So you see here the organic relationship in modern terms between democracy and liberalism. Liberalism, as the guarantee of certain essential freedoms for the individual, can exist without a democracy. You have had monarchies—the enlightened monarchies of the eighteenth century—where there existed a very great amount of freedom of speech, protection of the person, judicial guarantees of civil rights, and so forth. But obviously they did not have democracy. Because a ruler ruled by the grace of God; and the people not only had no influence upon the way he ruled, they had no influence on the identity of the ruler. But you cannot have democracy without liberalism. You cannot have democracy without minority rights. For democracy without minority rights is exactly a totalitarian democracy. Or as Aristotle puts it, "an autocracy." For this reason Aristotle makes this emphatic—puts great emphasis upon the prerequisite of laws for the democratic process. That is to say, you have to have laws. You have to have an objective order that is impartial, or at least its application approximates impartiality, in order to protect the minority from the unlimited rule of the majority. The very essence of democracy is that the minority of today has a legitimate constitutional chance to become the majority of tomorrow. And the majority of today who tomorrow is reduced to a minority has a constitutional guaranteed legitimate chance to become the majority again the day after. Where you don't have this you may have a plebiscitary dictatorship. You may have totalitarianism. But you don't have a democracy.

Of course they are intermediate stages where you can't tell exactly what kind of democracy is present. The same is true on a more general plane of the location of sovereignty. There are situations where the factorial distribution of power is so uncertain that you really can't tell. When did Bangladesh become a sovereign state? That is a question of empirical judgment, which under certain conditions is very difficult to make. The same is true of the degeneration of democracy into Fascism. When did it actually happen? At what point? I don't think anyone can say when it did actually happen. You have an accumulation of instances where the rights of minorities are habitually violated, where the dynamic process of democratic rule and challenge to that rule within the limits of the law no longer operate. At that point you arrive at the conclusion that the democratic forms still exist, but they have been emptied of content. You have the classic example in the transformation of the Roman Republic into an empire. Karl Loewenstein of Amherst has written a brilliant article on this transformation when Augustus retained and even re-emphasized the constitutional functions of the Senate, the Parliament, and the aristocratic Parliament, while allocating to himself all the substantive powers of the State.[1] That is to say, the titles he accepted were all the Republican titles, but they were now concentrated in the hands of one man and there was no effective counterweight against his powers. And so, after a while the Roman citizens could say, "We still have the Republican forms, but we have no longer the substance of Republicanism. We live in an empire and a monarchy." So you are correct, this is a transitional period where you can't be sure, and also you can't be sure of the restorative powers of democracy. During the McCarthy period you could say that democracy had in good measure ceased to operate, along with the liberal guarantees of individual freedoms. But at that time American democracy showed enough

---

1. I have been unable to locate the article to which Morgenthau refers here.

vitality to overcome this disease—it was a temporary disease. It could have been an endemic disease.

Student: But the point about democracy that the people should be able to change a bad ruler, that seems impossible in the United States today. In other words, the people can change the ruler only superficially, but in substance they will continue to be ruled by the same power.

HJM: What you are saying is the central distribution of power in the United States has not been affected by the succession of reform movements from Populism to the New Deal, to the New Frontier, to the Great Society. I happen to agree with you.

Student: Haven't the terms "minority" and "majority" become slippery, that is, you can make them have more substance by seeing them in terms of a class content. For example, let's say there's a hypothetical revolution in which a slaveholding regime is overthrown. The minority are slaveholders, and that minority then would not have the right to come back and take power again without making themselves a counterrevolution. In other words, it would not be built into the process that anybody who wants to can make slavery return. Whereas you might say those who have overthrown slavery may develop differences about other issues in which there will be a minority and a majority. But it seems to me, the way you have defined totalitarianism, every successful revolution is necessarily totalitarian in the sense that it means to put out of power, permanently, the few, the power elite, or whatever you want to call it, that have heretofore ruled.

HJM: We are talking about two different things. We are not talking about revolution. We are talking about the exact opposite, democratic continuity, democratic legitimacy. Certainly a revolution can only succeed permanently if it eliminates in one way or the other the old ruling class, and the organization of violence that was at the disposal of the ruling class. This was the point of difference between Kerensky and Lenin. Kerensky tried to rule with the influence of violence of czarism. You had the same in Germany in 1918. The congenital disease of the German Republic was that as soon as the Social Democrats came to power, they called upon the remnant of the Imperial Army to protect them against the Communists. And as Mao said, and he didn't invent the idea, "Political power comes out of the barrel of a gun." When the chips are down, that is the decisive element—who is it that controls the organization of violence.

Another central issue is whether it makes any difference who controls the Senate when you are dealing with the fundamental distribution of power in the United States. I say this with regret and it took me some time to learn it from experience, but if you look at the history of the great reform movements from Populism to the Great Society—which were all aiming at loosening or destroying the stranglehold that "the malefactors of great wealth" (as Theodore Roosevelt called them) exert upon American society—and if you look at the result, these movements have smoothed the edges of the issues, they have taken a little piece out here and there, but in essence the powers that be have remained in a state of surprising and impressive stability.

Another question arises as to how relevant have those reforms been for the control or the redistribution of power? Take, for instance, the so-called regulatory commissions that were established for the purpose of controlling monopolies or oligarchies—or the Interstate Commerce Commission controlling the railroad. All anti-trust laws. The regulatory commissions to an overwhelming extent have become the executive committees of the industries they were supposed to control. Look at the relations between the antitrust divisions of the Justice Department and ITT [International Telephone and Telegraph]. So you see there are certain things you can do with the ballot; there are other things you can't do with the ballot. And if the ballot were ever to threaten the monopolistic position of the concentrations of private power, and I include labor unions in that, you would probably get the abrogation of democracy. Those concentrations of private power, while really private governments, are a kind of new feudalism and are infinitely more powerful than the feudal lords of the Middle Ages were. And they would rather get rid of democracy than allow democracy to get rid of them.

Student: In the case of Chile, would that be a case of a minority becoming a majority—couldn't something like that conceivably happen in the United States?

HJM: I don't believe it could happen in the United States because the whole ethos of the United States would run counter to this kind of radical takeover by the state of industry. Also, it is an open question whether the Allende[2] experiment will succeed. There are very few if any instances of a radical change in the social and economic structure of a country that has been accomplished by consent, by democratic means. There are a few; surely Great Britain is perhaps a case, the Scandanavian countries, but by and large the powers that be have fought back, and at the expense of democracy. And, of course, in Chile the powers that be are not in the economic sense by any means as strong as the powers that be in this country.

Student: Do capitalist and communist economics at some point converge?

HJM: The convergence theory has a point on the technological level. There is no capitalist or communist way of mass-producing motorcars. There is only a competent way. The ideology of the bureaucrat who organizes mass production is irrelevant. But when it comes to the problem of scarce resources and the distribution and consumer choices, certainly there is a basic difference between capitalism and communism. Furthermore, and this goes back to what I said before, where the government assumes a monopoly not only of power but of truth and virtue as well, in the name of which it assumes that absolute power, you have no possibility for the people at large to have any influence on the assignment of resources and bureaucratic and economic decisions. You then have an absolutely autocratic state—as you have in the Soviet Union—with an enormous corruption and

---

2. Salvador Allende (1908–1973) was elected as president of Chile in 1970. As a socialist, he undertook progressive reforms in Chile, reforms that generated hostility from opponents both in Chile and in the United States. He died on September 11, 1973, in the midst of a coup d'état. Evidence about his death remains cloudy, although many believe he was assassinated by U.S.-backed agents.

distortion of the human personality. Everybody has to lie and to appear somebody different than they actually are. I have found this with my contacts with Russian intellectuals, for instance. It's most disturbing, the habitual lying in what we would call the most shameless way. I remember I had an encounter with a young historian, an academic who was supposed to be one of the most promising young historians and a very intelligent man. He told me, for a couple of hours, stories about the Soviet Union that were really hard to take. I asked a man, an American, who is of Russian origin and who is a great friend of those people and speaks Russian fluently, "Is he so ignorant or is he lying?" And he said, "Of course, he is lying."

Student: I think Marx was correct in saying that it is not the machine that is at fault but the way in which the machine is used; that is, the ownership of the machine.

HJM: But it is also the mechanics of the machine. Do you remember watching the faces and bodily movements of workers at the assembly line? You realize it is the assembly line that transforms the men into the appendages of the machine. I have seen it in the slaughterhouses of Chicago when a man would make one incision on the carcass of a pig continuously for eight hours a day—looking like an animal himself. And, of course, then afterwards going on a rampage, because who can stand that?

Student: I think there is a difference. You said they were the same mass production whether they were communist or capitalist. There seems to me this difference, that in a capitalist production, the main thing is profit before all, which means a continual speed-up of the assembly in which the workers have always to work faster. I am suggesting that this speed-up is inherent in capitalist production but not in socialist.

HJM: It is not? What about the hero of labor who has transcended the work norm by 35.7 percent?

Student: I said socialist, with which I don't equate the Soviet Union.

HJM: Well, then you are talking about something that doesn't exist yet.

Student: I am talking about something theoretical.

HJM: All right, then. I have nothing to contribute to the discussion. (Laughter)

Student: I am talking about an organization of production in which the workers themselves control the production, which I would call Socialism, in which they would decide how much is to be automated and how much they want to slow down, and so forth.

HJM: Let us assume that such a society exists. It is still a question considering the inner dynamics of mass production whether a society of worker-owners could transcend those dynamics. I would doubt that.

Student: I think the last point is an essential point both in regard to the difference between what Aristotle is calling for and what we are experiencing, and also the difference between one kind of assembly line and another, and that is the essential thing of participation in that process. It seems to me that Aristotle calls for face to face coming together of the many in order to make certain basic decisions about their lives, and we don't have that in our country to any large degree at all.

HJM: The town meeting comes closest to it.

Student: But when the town council of a large city in America meets, it's not the people coming together face to face. In an assembly plant, true, the process itself dehumanizes people—and I speak as one who worked five years on an assembly line. The process itself dehumanizes, but the degree to which the workers there have some say about it is a very essential point.

HJM: I can see that. In other words, the individual is reduced to an object, to becoming an appendage of the machine. We come to this when we discuss revolution in Book 5. One of the fundamental changes that has occurred in politics in the relations between the government and the governed is the technical impossibility of popular revolution in a technologically advanced country. A hundred years ago, there was an approximately equal distribution of material power between the government and the people. If the people could no longer stand the government, they could pull out their rifles from under their beds or from out of their closets and go into the streets and start shooting. The question then was who had more rifles, who had a better organization, better leadership, better morale, and that decided the issue. When the Spaniards wanted to get rid of the French in 1808, they did exactly that. They went into the streets and killed Frenchmen. A little more than a hundred years ago when the South refused to comply with the policies and laws of the federal government, they went to war. The question, the issue of slavery, was probably not more burdensome to the South then than the issue of integration and racial equality was to the South ten or fifteen years ago. But when Little Rock started to revolt, the President sent a division of the Army to Little Rock and that was it. And when Governor Faubus defied the government, the government reacted, and not even with force, and Faubus collapsed. The same happened with Wallace.[3] So the government today has a full monopoly or at least a quasi monopoly of the most effective technologies of transportation, communication, and warfare, and the people at large are completely helpless in the face of that unprecedented concentration of power. As long as that concentration of power is cohesive, it is not in itself riven by revolutionary forces. It is unchallengeable, and this is something that has not happened in history before. For this reason Hitler and Mussolini were overthrown not by their people but by foreign armies.

Student: Did you say the government has a monopoly on transportation, communications, and warfare?

HJM: Certainly. And a quasi monopoly on propaganda. I mean the impact that the government can have upon mass media. You may say unconscious adaptation

---

3. Orval Eugene Faubus (1910–1994) served as governor of Arkansas from 1955 to 1967. He came to national prominence when he defied the federal government's demand to desegregate the Arkansas public schools, leading to the confrontation at Little Rock (1957–1959). George Wallace (1918–1998) served as governor of Alabama and ran for president in 1968 and 1972. He gained national prominence for his 1963 refusal to allow black students to attend the University of Alabama.

of the mass media to the preferences of the government. You don't need censorship. You just need to know what is good for you.

Student: You just said provided that the apparatus itself doesn't become infected by this process. Isn't that precisely what happens in a genuine revolutionary situation—it doesn't overlook the people who are communications workers and workers in transportation and workers in armaments factories, workers who happen to be soldiers, etc. These people are not left untouched.

HJM: That depends. If you are considering the enormous effectiveness of modern technology, you need a very small number of people to man those technologies and put them into operation. Even a general strike could be broken if the Army remains faithful to the government. And here the American problem arises of a professional army versus a draft army. A draft army cannot be an instrument of a coup d'etat or of a counterrevolutionary policy because the draft army is, however incompletely, a reflection of the people at large. As I said earlier, if an American general would call upon his division to march on Washington and take over the government, they would string up the general at the next lamppost. Because most members of the army, as some of you will remember, hate the army. And there is no esprit de corps with the army that could be used for such an illegitimate purpose. But if you have a professional army you get a pressure group, a state within the state that has its own interests, its own ethics, its own cohesion. And this is a very dangerous thing.

Student: Is it true in general about the professional army that they always prove to be a pressure group that could be a problem. I was thinking in terms of England in the nineteenth century, when they did have a kind of professional army and it never was a problem.

HJM: Did they? A professional army in the nineteenth century? I remember very vividly the debates in the House of Commons about having a permanent police force. Peel suggested a police force and there was an outcry to the effect that this would be the end of democracy in Great Britain, because you cannot have (this was the liberal democratic position) a permanently armed group of people organized under unified command without those people abusing their powers and frightening and pressuring and coercing the civilian, unarmed population.[4] There was no standing army in Great Britain in the nineteenth century. Furthermore, to this day the British police do not carry firearms. And there is a profound truth in this—any organization of violence in the state performs a particular function for the distribution of power in that state. A completely neutral armed force within the state is a contradiction in terms. That is to say, a police force has to defend the status quo. That is its business. That is what law and order means.

Student: You said we couldn't have democracy without liberalism?

HJM: I say it again and again and again.

---

4. Sir Robert Peel (1788–1850) created the first modern police force in the United Kingdom in 1829 while serving as Home Secretary. The police were first called "bobbies" as a result of Peel's role in creating the institution.

Student: Isn't this by definition—isn't it a condition of democracy that we do have a guarantee of certain freedoms . . . ?

HJM: Yes, but frequently, even typically, we define democracy as government with the consent of the people. As I have said before, by that definition Nazism clearly was a democratic machine. So there must be—there is another type of democracy, which contains the liberal safeguards that thereby make changes in the rulers through constitutional means, through rational means, possible. So liberalism is inherent in democracy only if you define democracy in terms of liberal democracy. But if you define it in terms of plebiscitary democracy or simply the rule of the majority without qualification, then liberalism is not essential. You can have liberalism without democracy, but you can't have democracy without liberalism.

To Aristotle, law is an expression of objective truth sanctified by tradition.[5] It acts as a symbol of unity for those governed under it. If a code of law or a constitution is continually amended, it becomes no more than a series of legislative enactments beholden to majority decision. Conversely, a reluctance to change a law whose substance is unjust will create a diminished respect for all law. Aristotle pragmatically suggests change of law but not excessive change.

The reluctance to change the American Constitution underlies its function as a traditional symbol of unity for the American people. The Constitution has weaknesses, one major one being the lack of a parliamentary system that results in a lack of adequate congressional control over the executive branch of government. Despite the activities of the Center for Democratic Studies at Santa Barbara in drawing up a new constitution to rectify present weaknesses, no new constitution can be adopted. For America has no other uniting ties save the permanence of the Constitution.[6] Unlike other countries, America has no common history or tradition. Her population formed from waves of immigrants. She has no predestined geographical union, artificially grafting on to the territory of the original thirteen colonies. Nor does she have a dynastic continuity or an ethnic homogeneity. Thus, the basis of American citizenship and nationhood is a voluntaristic one. The dissatisfied can leave and renounce this American affiliation, an unheard of practice in the more stable countries of Britain and France. Unlike Britain, where a tradition of aristocracy serves as a force for stability and continuity, prompting Burke to speak of a British constitution since time immemorial, America has no such aristocratic tradition except for the antebellum South. In a sense, in America everyone is a liberal for there is nothing to conserve.

Some of the underdeveloped countries of the world share with America, to a greater degree, this attempt at substitution of a constitutional symbol of unity in the absence of other more meaningful unifying properties. Many of these countries

---

5. This section begins the seminar from November 27, 1970.
6. I have not been able to locate information on this center, which no longer seems to exist.

are creations of arbitrary colonial geographic limitations: Indonesia, consisting of thousands of Islands, is an artificial creation of the Dutch colonial policy. Throughout Africa, tribal frictions among "fellow citizens" of artificially created nation-states have led to wide scale occurrences of genocide.

In America the artificiality of her nationhood has historically manifested itself in the psychological need to assert the realness of her nationhood. The forming of the Know Nothings, the fighting of the Civil War, and the patriotic waving of the flag are all outward manifestations of the artificial attempt by Americans to assume an American nationhood.

In France we see the phenomenon of flag ostentation in a similar vein, serving as a unifying stabilizing substitute for the French governmental and constitutional instability. Countering the unsettling changeability of the governments of France, the French find the immutability of the symbol of her nationhood.

Can a nation change? There is the empirical continuity of the nation—the history, culture, national identity, character, psychology. Louis Philippe was different than Napoleon—a different legal entity—and in Russia, the Czar from the Bolsheviks. Does the new state succeed to the obligations of the old one?

In Book 3, Aristotle conceives of [the constitution] of the nation not in empirical terms but in rational legal terms. To him the nation is an artificial legal creation of the people. In America, for example, the president who acts in the nation's name can be compared to the officer of the legal corporation, while the citizens who share in both the responsibilities and privileges of the nation can be compared to the stockholders in a corporation. As in a legal corporation there is a continuity of the nation as a legal union though its members change. Change of government is a more ticklish question; but as an accepted principle of international law, successive governments are responsible for incurred "non-political" debts of the previous government. In a similar vein, Ernst Renan states, "The existence of a nation is an everyday plebiscite; it is, like the existence of the individual, a perpetual affirmation of life."[7] A perfect example of his meaning is provided in the case of the people who though of Polish origin, declared themselves Germans and thus became Germans. According to our definition of nation, "marginal minorities" may reside in one nation, since they identify themselves with other than the predominant national group of that nation.

I want today to attack seriously Book 4 of *The Politics*, which we started to discuss last time.[8] I pointed to the extraordinary practical wisdom of Aristotle, the lack of dogmatism and, more particularly, the attention to social conditions as

---

7. Ernest Renan, "Qu'est-ce qu'une nation?" [1882], reprinted in John Hutchinson and Anthony D. Smith, eds., *Nationalism* (Oxford: Oxford University Press, 1994).

8. The following section is from seminars dated March 21, 1972, in which Morgenthau turns to Book 4, where Aristotle develops more fully the distinctions between types of government. Morgenthau uses this section as an opportunity to consider whether or not a democracy, particularly the U.S. democracy, could devolve into fascism.

determining the nature of the political system. You can have a democratic constitution and—according to the character of the population, the distribution of power within society, the nature of society—you may have entirely different types of political systems, while the constitutional front remains exactly the same. This is for us an obvious insight. But if you consider attempts in the past to export democratic constitutions or democratic institutions to make South Vietnam democratic or Egypt under the British and so forth, you realize that the failure of those attempts has been the result of the neglect of this basic insight. The living constitution is a result of interplay of constitutional restrictions, institutions, and social forces, and the social forces are most important.

We have in the United States a constitution that is essentially the same as it was 150 years ago. But certainly the kind of political system we have today is utterly different from the one that existed 150 years ago. Because social forces have arisen, social forces have filled the empty spaces of the U.S. Constitution and have taken hold of the institution and have created something quite different from the political system that we had in the first third of American history.

An example might also be Wilson's attempt to make the world safe for democracy; you may have democracy or may not have democracy. Or you may have a very particular kind of democracy, utterly different from which we are accustomed. In the case of Vietnam, obviously the conception of elections determining the political system and the distribution of power in the state, the idea of national self-determination—these are concepts that have been taken from the Western countries and have been put in the context of Vietnam. You have a presidential system, you have a judicial system, you have a two-house legislature, and those institutions perform functions in South Vietnam utterly different from the ones they perform in the United States or in Great Britain or in Germany or France.

The important issue—important for our contemporary political powers—that Aristotle raises in the fourth book concerns the lowest type of democracy out of the five types that he distinguishes, a democracy that is identical with autocracy. This is an insight that had an illuminating effect upon the distinction and the similarity in certain respects between modern democracy and modern totalitarianism. It is exactly the transformation of the democratic order under certain conditions that has led historically to totalitarianism. It is a complete misconception both of the nature of totalitarianism and of the historical causation of totalitarianism to think that the concentration of governmental power, the government becoming stronger and stronger, will finally lead to a highly centralized, all-powerful totalitarian government. This has been the argument against concentration of power in Washington.

I am not here raising the general question as to whether this concentration of power in Washington is inevitable—is beneficial or not beneficial. In any event, the argument that has been typically raised against it is fallacious. For totalitarianism, especially if you think of its German and Italian examples, has not grown out of a concentration of power in the hands of the government so that the government amasses more and more power until finally it is in the full possession of it. To the contrary, it has been the result of weak governments, of governments that were unable to govern and were replaced through the democratic process with people, with movements, and charismatic leaders who promised, first of all, that they would govern. You have the beginning of a similar situation in this country insofar as parties and individuals run on the platform of law and order. They are not running on a *substantive* platform—social welfare, taxation, or whatever. They essentially run on a *procedural* platform. "We are going to govern! We are going to make the streets safe!" This is just as Mussolini got rid of the beggars on the steps of the churches and made the trains run on time. To make the trains run on time is part of order. And it is exactly with this slogan, with this promise, that totalitarian movements have come to power. They come to power not in contradiction of popular aspirations. It was not the typically nineteenth century liberal juxtaposition between the government and the people, so that what the government took away the people would lose. In those instances the concentration of power in the hands of the government was concomitant with the loss of popular power. To the contrary, the German and Italian movements were brought to power by popular movements, by democratic movements.

In the Soviet Union, of course, you have a different situation because you didn't have democracy before Bolshevism came to power. So you cannot really take the example of either Franco's Spain or the Soviet Union. The Bolshevist regime arose out of the Russian civil war, and in Spain democracy existed but it was destroyed from within and without during the Spanish civil war. Franco set up his particular type of totalitarian state instead.

When you think of the threat to American democracy that it may become a fascist type of democracy, then what you have to worry about is not that the government takes on too much power but that it is unable and unwilling to perform the functions that we expect a democratic government to perform. You have only to look at the appeal of Wallace, which is no longer primarily racial but which is exactly native fascist. Because Wallace says: "The politicians are crooks; they are liars; they have lied to you continuously; they steal your money; look at taxation; they rob you of your savings, look at inflation; they make a mess abroad; they make a mess at home; crime is rampant on the streets; they don't govern; I am going to govern." It is as simple as that. And if there are enough people dissatisfied, or if enough people find his argument plausible (and there are lots of people who find it plausible—myself included) and they don't think any further (which I certainly will do), they will put this kind of primitive demagogue into power. The saving grace of native American Fascism has been that it has generally brought to the fore very stupid and incompetent people, the present incumbent not excluded.[9]

---

9. George Wallace was, at the time of this seminar, running for president (1972). The incumbent to whom Morgenthau refers is Richard Nixon.

One might also consider the case of Joseph McCarthy.[10] He had one idea, which he got from a theologian—the late Father Walsh, the head of the School of Foreign Service at Georgetown University. McCarthy had lunch with him in 1948 or 1949 and he asked, on what platform should I run, and Father Walsh, who was a very sly, rather unpleasant gentleman whom I had the pleasure of meeting a couple of times, said communism.[11] And Joe McCarthy ran on the platform of anticommunism. He didn't know anything else. If McCarthy had had brains, if he had had any organizational talent, if he could have appealed to more than the fear of communism, if he hadn't been this kind of a one-issue man, he would have gone far. In all likelihood Wallace was in a different way more capable than McCarthy, but he was also not very capable. So this has really been the saving grace. And a man like Huey Long, who was capable, happened to be shot. So we have been lucky so far. (Laughter)

You can imagine a government assuming more and more powers—in other words, superceding the courts and legislature—and making the White House the center of power. You could visualize fascism developing that way. But it is still true it hasn't happened that way. And it is also true that the psychological forces that point toward fascism are a result of a profound malaise and dissatisfaction—I should say a profound and widespread malaise and dissatisfaction with the political status quo. That the regime, the old system is discredited and people want to get rid of it. They want a substitute for it. This is not the mechanism that you have in mind. Theoretically, what you have said is possible and one can imagine, let me say, a charismatic leader (a Napoleonic type) being elected president of the United States, who gets rid of the system of checks and balances. So you see, theoretically that's possible, technically that's possible, but morally that's very unlikely. Because why should the people at large allow such a president to ride roughshod over the Constitution and over the institutions of American government? And why should the legislature and the courts buckle under to such a charismatic leader? Where there is a popular ground swell that tries to get rid of the status quo and establish something new, you have an entirely different situation, because then the moral impetus is on the side of the people. But where you have a power hungry, ambitious charismatic leader, why should all the organs of government and the people at large abdicate and surrender their liberties to him? It's theoretically possibly, but historically it's unlikely.

I do not want to delve too deeply into fascism. I was only pointing to a very specific insight of Aristotle that is applicable to the contemporary situation. Surely fascism is an infinitely more complex phenomenon if you look at it as a totality. It is certainly true that fascism or totalitarianism—and this includes the

---

10. Joseph McCarthy (1908–1957) served as U.S. senator from Wisconsin and chaired hearings on communist infiltration of the U.S. government.
11. The story of the interaction between Fr. Edmund A. Walsh, S. J. and Senator Joseph McCarthy is told by David Halberstam in *The Best and the Brightest* (New York: Penguin 1972), 146–147. However, I cannot be certain that this is Morgenthau's source for this interaction.

Soviet Union and Spain—is an attempt to reintegrate a disintegrating society whose autonomous, indigenous social forces are no longer capable of providing that integration. You had it in the United States before the Civil War—you may get it again tomorrow or the day after. Where you get this, society tends to disintegrate into its component factors. In other words, the disintegrative factors are stronger than the integrative ones. This is always the case when vital interests are at stake, with which large masses of the population are identified. When these interests can no longer be compromised, when they can no longer be accommodated by the present political structure, then the political structure breaks down. In other words, democracy is only possible when the most vital issues facing a particular society have been settled at least to the moderate satisfaction of the main factors—of the main groups within society. You are not going to submit a vital interest on which your life, your honor, your pursuit of happiness, and what not depend to a majority vote. You are going to submit to majority vote only issues with regard to which you can tolerate a negative outcome. For this reason, nations don't submit political dispute to international jurisdiction. They are not going to allow control over those issues to slip from their hands and then be put into the hands of foreigners. Fascism imposes an order from above, a moral and social and political and economic order, which society is no longer capable of supplying from within its own indigenous forces. And it imposes this order through the modern technologies of transportation, communications, and war. And for this reason we can call it totalitarian.

It brings irresistible power to bear upon an essentially helpless people. And it uses both propaganda and terror and the incentive of having an honorific position within the context of a new integrative society. I think the class issue is also, of course, important. For you find in Germany, Spain, and Italy a very similar situation in which a capitalistic class and a land-owning class threatened in their most vital interests, their economic interests, tried to use the fascist organization, especially of paramilitary armed troops, as a shield against what they regard to be the rising proletariat. So the French capitalist could say, rather Hitler than Blum.[12] Rather a German fascist than a French socialist. I just happened to read this afternoon in a book on Max Weber that in 1918 Weber comments in a letter that there are German capitalists who would rather see the French in Germany, the French occupation of Germany, than to allow the Socialists to stay in power.[13] So this is certainly another factor that has led to the rise of fascism.

Finally we have, of course, not only the glorification but also the deification of nation. Here you have an atomized society in which the individual is a cog in the machine, an extension of the assembly line, and all of a sudden he becomes a member

---

12. Leon Blum (1872–1950) was a socialist member of the French parliament who served two brief terms as prime minister from 1936 to 1938. He was arrested by the Nazis when they invaded France and held prisoner until 1945.

13. I have not been able to discover the book to which Morgenthau refers here.

of the Master Race. Or a citizen of the new Roman Empire. Or of the Fatherland of Socialism. All of a sudden this powerless, atomized individual looks in the mirror at the uniform and he has a position, and he looks for somebody he can kick around. He may be kicked around by lots of people above him but there are a few below that he can also kick around. And this is great. Since the question has been raised, these are certainly the main functions of fascism. But what is interesting theoretically is how easily a democratic order can transform itself into a fascist order—into what you might call the exact opposite. Or at least, it is something quite different.

For one also has to consider when one deals with fascism that in all the major fascist systems of our age, there has been a very strong popular support for the systems. It is one of those errors that we are prone to commit to think of Franco or Hitler or Mussolini or even Stalin—and especially Castro, if you remember the Bay of Pigs—as dictators who rule an unwilling people. A people who can be deprived of their power, who can be overthrown very easily by sending thousands of refugees into Cuba. The people will rise and overthrow Castro. Castro is absolutely nothing of the kind. Castro is the exponent of a large, probably a majority consensus of the Cuban people. I am not raising as a question how that consensus has been achieved, but he is certainly not a traditional dictator ruling like the late Duvalier[14] over an unwilling people. He is, in a sense, a charismatic leader with a democratic base. That this base is democratic only in the sense that he rules with the consent of a large segment, if not of the majority, of the people, is of course, true. But what makes it a plebiscitary democracy, rather than a liberal democracy, is that once this plebiscitary democratic autocratic regime has been established, there isn't any way of disestablishing it. In other words, what is essential for democracy, what Aristotle would call polity, is the ability of the people to change their rulers through a rational constitutional process. If you don't like to be ruled, if the majority doesn't want to be ruled by this man or this group of men, it can get rid of that ruling group, not by killing them or making revolution, but by voting them out of office. Which is an extraordinarily civilized way of changing the government. In a totalitarian country you haven't got that ability. The ruler will continue to rule with the consent of the people because he is capable of manufacturing this consent through his monopoly of modern technologies. Whatever the popular origins of his power might have been, once he is in power he cannot be dislodged by rational constitutional means.

One might also consider the British system. You haven't got judicial control, you haven't got a separation between the executive and the legislative, and the House of Commons is sovereign. It has been said the House of Commons can do anything, except make a man into a woman. But the other set of principles is, of course, essential. And this is civil rights. Without liberal safeguards, you cannot

---

14. François Duvalier (1907–1971), known as "Papa Doc," became president of Haiti in 1957 and declared himself "president for life" in 1964. His son, Jean-Claude Duvalier, also known as "Baby Doc," continued his father's dictatorial rule from 1971 to 1986 when he was overthrown in a popular uprising.

have democracy. Liberalism in the sense of civil rights is essential for the democratic order. You can have liberalism without the democratic order as you had in the enlightened absolutism of Frederick the Great, Francis the Second of Austria, and so forth. You can have liberalism without democracy, but you cannot have democracy without liberalism. In other words, without freedom of speech, without freedom of assembly, without freedom of the press, without freedom from unreasonable seizures and searches, without the whole plethora of the first ten amendments to the Constitution, you cannot have democracy. Because if you don't have those laws in the Aristotelian sense, the majority of today will transform itself into a permanent majority, which leaves no opportunity for the minority to become the majority through rational constitutional processes. For this is exactly the mechanism of democracy. That not by somebody's whim, not by somebody's will, but by virtue of the objective laws of the land the majority of today can become the minority of tomorrow and the minority of today can become the majority of tomorrow through a system of a transformation based upon the popular will. Where you don't have this, where you don't have it effectively, where you don't have this at all, you don't have democracy. And where you don't have it effectively, you have a democracy in crisis.

Student: Do you recognize the use of the term democracy in the expression "economic democracy" as the Soviet Union might use it?

HJM: No, because this is mere ideology. What is economic democracy—that we vote here what price we are going to pay for a cup of coffee downstairs? I know historically what economic democracy was supposed to have meant—the workers deciding their own norms, their own conditions of work, their own quantity of production, and so forth. But that is like the army. There are certain branches of human activity that simply don't lend themselves to democratic decision making, that are in essence elitist. In war you couldn't put the battle plan for tomorrow's battle to a democratic vote of the soldiers tonight and let the majority decide. The same is true of economic management. In the Soviet Union certainly management is based upon what is called "democratic centralism." And democratic is written in very small letters, and centralism is written with capital ones. This can't be otherwise. You may pretend that it is otherwise, but truly it can't be. You have an assembly line, what can you decide democratically? You can, of course, decide whether you should have a coffee break at 2 or 2:30 or if it should last ten minutes or fifteen minutes or whether you should have two days off every two weeks or every three weeks. But the basic economic decisions have to be made by an elite. By some people who have a certain competence and who bear a certain responsibility.

Student: The Soviet Union used to maintain that they had democracy, a truer democracy than the United States, and they cited the fact that they had economic equality . . .

HJM: That they have a truer democracy than the United States—this claim has much more profound roots than that they pretend that the people own the means of production, that production is done for the sake of the people, and so forth. This is a result of the claim that true democracy exists only in the Soviet Union and, more particularly, true freedom of the press exists only in the Soviet Union. It has a very profound root in the varied political philosophy of Marxism and Leninism. That is to say that you start with the assumption that you have, let me say, a politburo as the expression of the party, the leader of the party, the vanguard of the party, which has a monopoly of truth and virtue—that it is the authentic interpreter of the truth and virtue of Marxism and Leninism. It follows automatically that, for instance, what you read in *Pravda* and *Izvestia* is much superior to what you read in the *New York Times* and the *Washington Post*, which are allowed to print lies. *Pravda* and *Izvestia* are only allowed to print the truth. So why allow swindlers and crooks and incompetents to put their lousy opinions into print; in the Soviet Union, what you read is the truth. And naturally if the pretence is correct, then the Bolshevist system is superior to the democratic one.

Student: I think the point can be summed up under Marx that in every epoch the ruling ideas are the ideas of the rulers. They are the ones who have the means; that is, in a society like ours, the people that have the most money can produce the most *Daily News* and so on. It is clear that you can also put out your own little underground paper, but that is as far as the total social weight goes; it is miniscule compared to what they can put out.

HJM: But it is also true, isn't it, that lots of people have money but they don't all have the same interest in terms of class and in terms of political ideas? I know a few millionaires who have entirely different positions in the political spectrum. Now you may say in a capitalistic society that it makes really no difference whether you are in the right wing of the Republican party or in the left wing of the Democratic party. It is still a capitalistic system and those are minor differences within the capitalistic system. It all depends upon your perspective. If you look at the whole business from say, the Moon or Mars, the difference between communism, capitalism, and the Catholic Church may be completely irrelevant. It may all be essentially the same thing—earthlings who are engaged in their silly business. But if you look a little bit closer, especially if you come close to where the practical problems arise, I think you can see the fundamental difference between a political system that is based upon a revealed and essentially immutable truth, which is really a secular church and a pluralistic system, and one where (within certain limits, I grant you) all kinds of ideas can compete in the "marketplace of ideas," to use Mr. Justice Holmes' term again. I grant you not every idea can be propounded with an equal chance of being accepted; the competition is unequal. But there is a world of difference between living in a totalitarian country— intellectually operating in a totalitarian country—and living in a liberal democratic country. I have had close contact from time to time with Russian intellectuals and I have always been aghast by the moral corruption and the mutilation—intellectual and human mutilation—that this regime imposes upon its citizens, its intellectuals.

There is a beautiful statement of this in a little book on democracy by the Austrian political philosopher and constitutional lawyer Hans Kelsen.[15] He says that the difference between democracy and totalitarianism has been clearly revealed in the encounter between Christ and Pontius Pilate. Christ, the non-democrat, says, "I am the King of the Jews." And that's it. You don't have to put that to a democratic test. And Pontius Pilate, the relativist, asks the people, "Whom do you want, Barrabas or Jesus of Nazareth?" And the majority decides. The opinion hasn't been unanimous that the decision was correct (laughter) but that is democracy.

Take the statement of Cromwell[16] to the delegation of Scottish Presbyterians: "I beseech you by the bowels of Christ to think it possible that you might be mistaken." No member of the politburo will ever say this to his colleagues. Forget about the bowels of Christ. Nobody can even think of the possibility that he may be mistaken. He cannot be mistaken; he can only be a heretic. If he is unsuccessful or if his policies run counter to your interests—Chinese vs. the Soviet Union—then you are a traitor, a heretic. You have sold out to the capitalists. It is not that you are wrong within the system—that you have made a mistake or that your interests don't square with mine. Since I have a monopoly of truth and virtue, anybody who disagrees is a scoundrel, is a traitor, and is a heretic. And so you have between Moscow and Peking the same relationship that you had between Rome and Wittenberg during the Reformation.[17] Both claim that they are the repository of the Marxist/Leninist truth and virtue. And it can't be at both places at the same time—it has to be either here or there. In a democracy you assume—you start with a relativistic conception of truth and virtue. You believe in your own but you don't deny the possibility that the other side might also have a parcel of truth. And through the process of democratic elections, you give the other side a chance to make its claim prevail.

Certainly, for most people freedom of speech and freedom of the press is irrelevant because lots of people don't talk in any way that needs to be protected by the law. They say, "Good morning" or "How are things?" and so forth. And most people don't read, or read only the sports page. So what difference does it make whether the first page is censored as long as the last page gives you the results of yesterday's basketball game?

Student: You said where these civil liberties don't operate effectively you don't have a democracy. Where you have the civil liberties but they don't function

---

15. I believe the "little book" to which Morgenthau refers is Hans Kelsen, *Vom Wesen und Vert der Demokratie*, 2nd ed. (J.C.B. Mohr, 1929). The book, which is only 119 pages, does not appear to have been translated into English, although there is a German reprint from 1981.

16. Oliver Cromwell (1599–1658) was a leader in the British civil war who attained the title of lord protector in 1649. He ruled Britain for nine years. As a Puritan, Cromwell sought to convince opposing religious denominations to accept his views and rule, which explains the comment toward the Scottish Presbyterians, who were supporters of the monarchy at this time.

17. Morgenthau refers to the dispute between Martin Luther and the Vatican. Wittenberg is the home of Luther.

effectively you have a democracy in crisis. I think at the root of this question is whether they operate effectively in the United States. That is, if it is true that most people don't read, then what is the value of having the freedom from some intellectual point of view?

HJM: Yes, but the minority that reads determines the intellectual and moral and political climate and, you may say, the fate of the nation. It is not the masses who do it but an elite. That is so here and elsewhere and has always been so. The only question is: What kind of elite? And under what restraints does it operate? And what are the rights of the people at large to control and to end this elite? But the fact that it is an elite which is in the minority is obvious.

Student: I would agree that the majority always has to have leadership. But would you say that civil liberties of the United States today are working in an effective democratic manner?

HJM: Well, they work in a somewhat diminished manner, but they still operate. Take myself with regard to the war in Vietnam. I have suffered certain disabilities. President Johnson has tried to get me, if you want to put it that way. But I haven't been sent to Alaska. I got an offer from the University of Alaska, and I was told that it was free of snow three months of the year. But I haven't been sent there by the FBI—they haven't come to me one morning and said, "Get ready, we go to Fairbanks."

Student: That is exactly the question. Until 1965 when things went well, the majority of the establishment who are disbelieving of the intellectual, of the academic, was willing to betray and to take the money from the government. It was only when things went wrong that they took a more critical attitude.

HJM: Obviously you don't take a critical attitude when everything is right. I mean, you naturally take a critical attitude when things go wrong.

Student: Why did you take a critical attitude in 1965 on the Vietnam War—why did you and a few other academics take an attitude that things were wrong?

HJM: It was a very small minority.

Student: Do you contend that the Aristotelian definition of constitutional democracy is incompatible with any form of socialism in a modern industrial state?

HJM: No. This is an entirely different issue.

Student: I think we have all been talking around this issue.

HJM: No. We haven't been talking around this issue. We have raised it. But that is an entirely different issue. Obviously you have a socialist economy in the Scandinavian countries—you have state ownership of the means of production, you have social security on a very large scale, you have socialist governments in most cases. It is one of those academic questions: What are the preconditions of democracy? And there are people who say that only in a free enterprise system can you have democracy. I don't see that at all. In other words, the economic arrangements of society are compatible with all kinds of political systems. Historically you will find certain arrangements in certain systems and other arrangements only in other systems, but logically, rationally there is no necessary relationship between a particular type of economic organization and a particular type of political organization.

Student: You mean a high concentration of wealth is compatible with democracy?

HJM: It is compatible with popular democracy—it depends very much on how that wealth is being used. You have a very high concentration of wealth in this country. And certainly the owners of great wealth have opportunities to influence the government that you and I haven't got. That is obvious. But it is always also true that in other countries, in different systems, for example where you have a theocratic state, obviously the representatives of the religious organization have a particular channel to the government that other individual citizens haven't got. Take the influence that certain universities had upon the government. In this country even the great influence of certain clergymen—I have mentioned Father Walsh before. He was the single most important factor in the personnel policies of the State Department. The graduates of the Georgetown Foreign Service School whom he recommended were automatically admitted. And people with certain strange foreign names were automatically excluded. So that certain groups or individuals in view of their particular social position within a particular social and political system have a disproportionate influence upon the government is inevitable.

In monarchical times (but not only in monarchical times), frequently it was the mistress of the prince, for instance, who had an inordinate influence upon policy. We talk here about the quantification of political science. This is an age-old attempt. In the seventeenth century, the eighteenth century, such attempts were made also on a quantitative, mathematical basis. For instance, in regard to the balance of power in the eighteenth century, people tried to quantify it completely. When Frederick the Great was acquainted with one of those schemes, he asked, "What is the quantitative equivalent of the influence which a mistress has upon the prince?" So this is inevitable, and this has nothing to do with democracy. When such influence becomes so strong that it becomes monopolistic or quasi-monopolistic, it reduces democracy to a farce. Because then the people who really rule are what Theodore Roosevelt called "the malefactors of great wealth"—and the people simply go through the motions of voting or ratifying or not ratifying certain legislative enactments.

Student: In what way does that essentially differ from what now happens here in the United States?

HJM: You have a point. It doesn't differ essentially but it still differs quantitatively. For insofar that a substantial minority of the people—take the busing issue today or the Vietnam war a couple of years ago—take a certain stand, the popularly elected representatives who want to be reelected will take that public position into account. They will take it into account the same way in which they take into account, say, the financial advantage that a great corporation promises or gives them. Or the disadvantages with which they threaten them. It becomes one factor among many. This is one of the dogmatic distortions of our political processes—that people have the tendency to isolate one factor and make it the solely important one. Take, for instance, our Middle Eastern policy, which is certainly influenced by what is generally called the Jewish vote. But this is by no means the only factor. The oil interests are another factor. Also, anti-Communist, anti-Soviet, and a great number of other factors are brought to bear upon the policy process. Which one will prevail or whether there will be a compromise, which is much more likely in our system, is an open question.

Student: But public opinion constrains decisions in both the U.S. and the Soviet Union.

HJM: But within much more narrow limits. Certainly the government of the Soviet Union can't afford continuing drastic food shortages. It has to do something about it because people are not going to work, they are going to slow down or they are going to make protest demonstrations. When you deal with other than a bunch of illiterate peasants, you have to take public opinion into account.

Student: From this relativistic point of view that we have in this country, apparently it wouldn't be possible to say that the Vietnamese war is absolutely wrong by any universal standards of morality?

HJM: Well, I have said this and I would say it again: I disagree with Mr. Nixon's policies. But I can understand them. And if his assumptions were correct, he might be successful. And there is a possibility that he might still be successful. It might well be that both the Chinese and the Russians would rather have an American presence in South Vietnam than a Russian or Chinese presence. Again, there is an irony in the whole development. I would still say I am right and he is wrong; but I can understand how a man sitting where he does, or a man like Rusk[18] whom I knew very well, can arrive at those conclusions. I wouldn't say that he was bought by the enemies of mankind or that he is a moral incompetent or a wolf in sheep's clothing—in any case that is beyond the pale.

Student: Would you say that he is a war criminal?

HJM: You raise another issue, that is, the applicability of the Nuremburg principles to a nation that has not been defeated. Because the peculiar thing about the Nuremberg trials, which I pointed out in 1946 in an article in *America,* is that it is the victor who imposes the principles upon the vanquished. One member of the court was a representative of Stalin, who was as much a war criminal as the others.[19] If you make aggressive war a crime, then certainly Hitler and Mussolini were war criminals, but so were Stalin and Molotov who, after all, planned aggressive war in August 1939. And if you look at the Kaytn massacre of the Polish officers, most certainly that was a war crime, too.[20] So that is a very ticklish question.

---

18. Dean Rusk (1909–1994) served as secretary of state for both John F. Kennedy and Lyndon Johnson, 1960–1968.

19. Hans J. Morgenthau, "Views of Nuremburg: Futher Analysis of the Trial and Its Importance," *America* (December 7, 1946): 266–267.

20. The Kaytn Forest massacre occurred in 1940 when Soviet forces executed more than 4,000 Polish officers. After the conclusion of World War II, the Soviets claimed that the Nazis had been responsible for the executions. In 1989, Mikhail Gorbachev admitted that it was Soviet forces who had committed the killings.

I think a war crime is essentially the vengeance wrought by the hypocritical victor upon the vanquished. You can't apply such a principle universally. I mean, if you were to apply it to the people responsible for the war in Vietnam, you would start with Johnson, McNamara, and Westmoreland and it would go down the line. Who is going to do that?

CHAPTER 4

Ethics and Politics

We discussed last time primarily the problem that has become famous because of Aristotle's treatment, and the problem concerns the relationship between the virtue of the good citizen and the virtue of a good man. Aristotle arrives at the conclusion that the two generally are not identical, and he arrives at this conclusion by virtue of the basic teleological conception of his general philosophy. That is to say, in his functions, the telos of a good citizen is not identical with the telos of a good man. A good man has a broader telos; he has to fulfill his destiny as a man while the good citizen has only to perform a limited function as a good citizen. There is one exception to this and that is the exception of the good ruler. The virtue of a good ruler is identical with the virtue of a good man. Because the good ruler, having to preside over a human society of which all human beings are members, must promote, since man is a political animal, the telos of man as such, and thereby his functions as a good ruler and his functions as a good man become identical. This is the Aristotelian version of the famous Platonic conception of the philosophers becoming kings and the kings being philosophers. That is to say, in the perfect state of a political commonwealth, the virtue of the good ruler becomes identical with the virtue of the good man. Which is, of course, an ideal situation that is not likely to occur in practice. So in practice there will always be a discrepancy between the virtue of the good man and the virtue of the good ruler. Now this Aristotelian conception is alien to our conception of morality or virtue,

This chapter includes Morgenthau's discussion of ethics through the prism of Aristotelian virtue ethics. These sections come from two different periods, December 1970 and February 1972. There is some overlap between the two lectures, so I have eliminated those sections that are repetitive. The first section is dated December 4, 1970, and appears to include notes from one of the students, Martin Price.

and we would not make this simple distinction that Aristotle makes. Why not? What is the basic difference in our philosophic assumptions and the Aristotelian ones that lead to quite disparate conclusions with regard to this basic problem of political morality?

The answer is that we have a dualistic conception of morality, a transcendent conception that is not inherent in the nature of man but is imposed upon man by supranational power. And the symbol of this dualism is Moses coming down from Sinai with the tablets of the law, seeing the children of Israel adoring the golden calf and smashing the tablets. This transcendental conception of morality is completely alien to Aristotle's way of thinking. Since we accept a moral code to which all men are subject, for us the problem of political morality poses itself in entirely different terms. In other words, we assume that all men are subject to the same moral principles regardless of their station within society, especially within a political society. This being so, we have to ask ourselves to what extent—and this is a question again which Aristotle doesn't raise, which is an empirical question—to what extent does the moral behavior, the morally relevant behavior of a citizen differ from the moral behavior of man in general? More particularly, to what extent does the moral behavior of a ruler differ from the moral behavior expected of a man in general?

One might ask if our society is really a Judeo-Christian one, but is not rather more relativistic. Let me respond by considering the problem of lying. We frown upon deliberate telling of untruths in our personal relations. If I would ask you a question, whatever it is, and you would tell me an outright lie, I would find it unacceptable on moral terms. In order to get to the heart of the issue, let's avoid extreme examples. If I ask you, "Have you got notes?" and you say, "No," and you have notes of the last lecture, I would resent it for personal reasons, and I would also resent it for moral reasons. But if a candidate for political office tells you outright lies, or if a politician in office tells you outright lies, you would not resent it. So, in other words, we operate on a dual morality in which what is allowed to the politician may not be allowed to the individual. Again, "If we had done for ourselves what we have done for Italy, what scoundrels we would have been." In other words, if we had done for our private purposes the misdeeds, the violations of the moral code, that we did for the sake of Italy, we would have been subject to moral disapprobation. But since we did what we did for the sake of Italy, no moral disapprobation applies to us. This is the problem of political morality as we see it today quite in contrast to Aristotle.

Student: I am really not sure that it is in contrast, because it seems to me that there are two things involved here. On the one hand, someone accepts a morality in which the ends justify the means. I brought up the question before of lying, say, for the sake of my own life. Similarly, someone accepts the fact that one may lie for political ends and, therefore, lying is acceptable under terms X, Y, and Z, which include politics and maybe starvation. On the other hand, however, if an individual accepts absolute moral standards in which lying is wrong, lying would be wrong just as well for the politician as for the individual. For Gandhi, violence would be just as wrong for him as an individual as violence in the name of the state.

HJM: Yes, but Gandhi is, of course, a case apart. You cannot draw general conclusions from Gandhi, whose opposition to violence was not as absolute as it appears in retrospect, especially to some less liberal interpreters. For Gandhi, nonviolence was the most convenient political tactic under the prevailing circumstances.[1]

Student: But what I am saying is that the people who will accept what we would call political immorality are those who don't really have an absolute moral standard. They have a relativistic moral standard. It's just a question of where the relativity lies.

HJM: Of course you can have an absolute moral standard. You say that lying under any circumstances is disapproved on moral grounds. Pacifists and Quakers believe that violence under any circumstances is wrong for moral reasons. But then you opt out of the political realm altogether.[2] You take a metapolitical position and say, "Politics is rotten on moral grounds and we have nothing to do with it, on moral grounds," which is, of course, the position of many alienated youths in this country today. Politics is a lousy business, a rotten business; we have nothing to do with it. We go back to nature, or go back to Woodstock, or whatever it is we go back to. In any case, we opt out of the political situation, as it exists. But this does not answer the question. It answers the question for certain individuals who have made an individual decision on moral grounds, but it is not an answer. It is like the hermit who goes into the woods and prays for the rest of his life.

Student: Isn't it an answer in the sense that we have moral standards that are not absolutely relativistic. Even if they're transcendental, they're relativistic. And since they are that way, all we do is say that for political questions the moral standards become much narrower.

HJM: This is correct, but you see, whether this is relativistic is an open question. It may be also what is now called in theological ethics "situational ethics." In other words, you have to ask yourself, "What is possible for the average man who is not a saint, who doesn't aspire to sainthood, under the concrete condition under which he lives?" This problem arises, of course, with particular acuteness in the

1. This may be a reference to Reinhold Niebuhr, who argued that Gandhi's nonviolence was actually a very coercive practice. See *Moral Man and Immoral Society* (New York: Charles Scribner's Sons, 1932), 241–249.
2. It is interesting to consider Morgenthau's position here in relation to Hannah Arendt's book, *On Violence*, which was published in 1972. She argues that violence is actually not in the political realm, the direct opposite of what Morgenthau is arguing here. Morgenthau and Arendt were friends, although it is not clear the extent to which their writings influenced each other's work. Morgenthau did write one article about Arendt, Hans J. Morgenthau, "Hannah Arendt on Totalitarianism and Democracy," *Social Research* 44 (spring 1977): 127–131. Arendt's *On Violence* is found in *Crises of the Republic* (New York: Harcourt Brace Jovanovich, 1972), 103–198. For their interactions with each other, see Elisabeth Young-Bruehl, *Hannah Arendt: For the Love of the World* (New Haven, CT: Yale University Press, 1982).

field of politics, but it arises in other fields as well. Because none of us has ever refrained from lying, I would suppose. Consider, for example, the physician who doesn't tell a terminal patient that he is going to die, who leaves him under the illusion that he is going to live. I have recently had a related experience. I have an infection of the lower jaw that is quite inconvenient, painful, not dangerous, but I have difficulty in talking and it's painful. The dentist never told me. I concluded from my own general knowledge of medicine and certain indications that this is what it was. You just take penicillin and this and that and the other. I asked him, "If I have nothing more than a toothache, why would I take all this?" This is the obvious conclusion. He didn't tell me for reasons that are perfectly honorable but are a violation of a basic principle, not even to tell an implicit lie. This is not relativistic; it is rather the adaptation of, let me say, the Ten Commandments to the concrete conditions under which men live. Because to comply with the Ten Commandments in the literal sense requires a total human goodness, a total virtue that is not attainable by the man in the street.

Take the problem of "Thou shalt not kill." There is nothing in the Ten Commandments that says: "In war you ought to kill as many enemies as possible." And there are, as we know, people who take this command literally, refuse to adapt it to circumstances, and are conscientious objectors on religious grounds. But the common run of men who have not such an acute moral sensitivity, kill and are morally excused for this because of the necessities of social life that make it inevitable for a man to kill under certain circumstances. Take the police. The police are trained to kill under certain circumstances. They don't walk around morally anxious, because this is what they are supposed to do.

Student: I think it's precisely because we have a set of values that is above human nature that we have to take this view of morality because, according to Aristotle, it's inherent in human nature to do certain things and it's possible for a person to be virtuous. But for us, since we do see dualism, we see an absolute standard and the human being has to adapt to it.

HJM: That's perfectly correct. You see, for this reason the Greeks were probably much happier than we are from a moral point of view. It was much easier for them to be moral than it is for us. Take the issue of deception. I read the other day passages from the *Odyssey* because somebody told me that the conception of the silent majority first appears in the *Odyssey*. That is to say, Odysseus going down to Hades says, "Here are the dead, the silent majority," which is a genuine silent majority. I don't know whether Mr. Agnew had read the *Odyssey* and got it from there.[3] I would, personally, doubt it. If you read the *Odyssey*, you see the continuous deception that takes place for good purposes. For example, the moving scene

---

3. Spiro Agnew (1919–1996) served as Richard Nixon's vice president from 1969 to 1973. He resigned in 1973 due to accusations of bribery. He was famous for attacking liberals and academics and for using the phrase "the silent majority" to refer to that element of the American public that did not openly protest administration policies, most particularly the U.S. war in Vietnam.

when Odysseus, after twenty years, meets his father, Laertes, and deceives him saying, "I am the son of so-and-so" in order to test him and see whether he still loves him. Or Penelope, who deceives everybody around her, who says she can't marry anybody because she must first finish her tapestry, and she continuously does her needlework and at night she unravels it so she starts all over again next morning.

In other words, you have in ancient Greece a situational ethics to begin with. You haven't got a transcendental ethics at all. So man can live in peace with himself on moral grounds much more easily as a Greek than as a member of the Judeo-Christian society. And this, of course, is as I said last time, the main argument of Nietzsche against Christianity.[4] That it tries to force man into a moral straightjacket that is against his nature. Take, in particular, sexual ethics. We have the suppression of natural drives, their perversion, and the creation of institutions to take care of the suppressed sexual drives is, of course, obvious. Which leads to deception, to immoralities that were completely alien to the Greeks. The Greeks did what came naturally and were very happy about it. The point I want to make again is that there exists a fundamental distinction between our conception of morality and the Greek conception and even other non-Judeo-Christian conceptions of morality.

I came across this a couple of years ago in Nepal. I met a Tibetan who had been a very prominent trader from Tibet to Nepal and India and who left when the Chinese came. He opened a hotel, still traveling to Tibet from time to time. He introduced me to his wife, whom I then thought was his only wife. Then he introduced me to another lady, a young woman in her early twenties, and he said, "That is also my wife." And I said, "Well, what's going on here?" I said it more politely. He said, "Well, the first wife couldn't bear me any children and so I had the problem of either getting rid of her and marrying another wife or to make some arrangement." The first wife had a niece to whom she introduced her husband and arranged the marriage. So he had three children from the young wife, the niece of the first wife, and they live together. I asked, "How do they get along?" He said, "Fine, I go to the movies on Monday with one wife, on Tuesday with the other wife." I don't know whether this was a mere metaphor, but in any event, they lived happily together. I said to myself, how much more natural and how much more sensible an arrangement this is than you would have in a Western country where this would create enormous moral, legal, and social problems, with unhappiness all around. Everybody was happy. He also said in passing that he has another wife in Lhasa and whenever he goes to Lhasa, he goes to the movies with her.

I'm not here propagating one against the other, but what is obvious is that the Judeo-Christian ethic imposes enormous constraints upon the individual and

---

4. For the influence of Nietzsche on Morgenthau's thought, see Christoph Frei, *Hans J. Morgenthau: An Intellectual Biography* (Baton Rouge: Louisiana State University Press, 2001).

creates enormous moral, social, legal problems that are avoided in societies that live under more natural moral codes. And the Greek moral code is one of them.

Student: There is just something about the whole idea that bothers me. It seems to me that what justifies deception or what we would consider immoral behavior in terms of the Greeks is the telos, is the end. You're realizing what you are naturally. But it seems to me that in realizing my end in these kinds of ways, there are other people's ends who aren't going to be realized. Consider the story of Odysseus, for example. They're not fulfilling what their end ought to be; therefore, their destruction is just, even though certain characters, if I recall, are painted in a sympathetic light. The point is, I don't think that's the way it is. That is, you have to start from the assumption that everybody's end is in harmony and the good guys then can do whatever they want to get rid of the bad guys, rather than the other assumption that really life is just a conflict between people.

HJM: Of course, you are entirely correct. What the Greeks didn't see, didn't want to see, was exactly this kind of dynamism that refuses to be put into teleological categories that are applicable from beginning to end and which, of course, more particularly are an instrument that justifies the *status quo*. The slave has his telos like the flute maker has his telos as over against the flute player. And so the citizen has a perfect right to use the slave for his purposes to perform certain subordinate functions, because if he had to perform them, he couldn't fulfill his own telos. But it is nowhere written in the stars or in innate human nature that what seems to be the telos of one man at a particular period of his life or because he is born into a particular station, is bound to remain his telos forever. The idea that a man who is born a slave can rise by his own efforts to become a free man or a ruler is, of course, alien to this kind of static conception of a well-ordered universe where everybody and everything has its natural place and you have only to define that natural place and everything else follows with necessity.

Take for instance the Napoleonic generals, who, in private life, included all kinds of people—bakers, shoemakers, traders—and who, because of the revolutionary destruction of all social barriers, which were regarded by the French aristocracy as natural barriers, rose to stations that formerly had been reserved to a particular small group of Frenchmen who thought that they had the natural right to rule because they were members of the aristocracy. So, the Aristotelian politics is a static one in which everything is preordained. Certainly, you can free a slave if he is worthy of it, but it depends upon your judgment, not upon the slave's ability. If you overlook the slave's ability, he will remain a slave. This is only true, of course, for legal slavery, not for natural slavery. For us, nothing is really predetermined and it is a matter of, you may say, the competition of life as to who is going to come out on top. I mean, here is Mr. Truman, a bankrupt haberdasher, a beneficiary of an utterly corrupt political machine, who becomes president of the United States—and if not in prospect, but certainly in retrospect, not the worst president we have ever had. This kind of idea is completely alien to the Greek mind that operates in a static, beautiful, well-ordered universe where everything and everybody has its place, its function, and there is no transcending those functions one way or the other.

Student: If you begin to get into it, what first looks like a very orderly, harmonious concept of the world really serves to justify the most tremendous kind of oppression of people. Even the sample you used of the man with three wives. Everybody was happy, except that there is a sense of a violation of the rights of people there in which, for example, women are seen as undoubtedly bearers of the race and nothing else. Sure, it's natural, but I react to that because it's almost an automatic reaction. If someone says it's natural, my reaction is, yes, but whose interest is it in? And what happens here is that a society propagates itself with very nice moral justification, but in the interests of certain people.

HJM: Yes, of course, then we would have to ask whether this is not always true and whether the real problem is then *qui bono?* In whose interest is it? You see, this is the conception of Marx, that throughout history all revolution serves the interest of a particular exploiting minority to the detriment of the majority. And in one revolution after the other, another exploiting minority replaces the existing exploiting minority. But the basic problem of exploitation, of the class division of society, of the minority rule remains. It is only in the proletarian revolution that the millennium is brought about where a revolution is made for the sake of the majority, and where minority rule exploitation itself and the class distinction of societies themselves are eliminated. But this is an eschatological, not an empirical conception. We have certainly seen that in the Soviet Union and in all so-called classless societies, socialist or communist societies, a new class arises, which continues the process of minority rule and exploitation. This is even true in the Christian eschatology of which, really, Marxism is a secularized version, that the Kingdom of God is not of this world, is not going to be brought about by political improvements but is going to be brought about at the second coming of Christ. Christ will come again and deliver the world and the day of last judgment will make an end to this world, as the world revolution will make an end to this world, and will usher in a new, morally untainted society. So, what you say, I think, is entirely correct.

But then this remains the question, the issue that politics cannot evade. That is to say, to whose advantage, in whose interest is this particular arrangement? And if there were a Women's Liberation movement in Nepal, obviously this arrangement would not endure. But since there is no such thing yet, it remains under the prevailing conditions of consciousness and interests, a perfectly acceptable and, I would say, honorable and decent arrangement that avoids social frictions and moral ambiguities and so forth.

Why is it that this man has three wives? Two of them he has for moral reasons. He didn't want to get rid of the first wife. Then he wanted to have children; that meant that he needed another wife. Then he went to Lhasa; he was lonely and he needed a third wife. And all those wives are perfectly happy. I don't know whether the Lhasa wife had other husbands, too; I didn't go into this. I didn't want to excite him. But in any event, the idea that women in such a society have the same rights as men runs counter to the functions that are assigned to women and that, of course, to a certain extent are there by biological condition.

Student: What about the first wife? She had the choice of being divorced or accepting the situation, but she was coerced. You don't get married just to have children. You're really excusing the rights of the first wife.

HJM: Then the question arises, you may get married even in Nepal not only for the purpose of having children, but certainly also for the purpose of having children. If your wife is unable to perform this main function of having children, one of the main functions for which you got married, and since adoption obviously doesn't exist . . .

Student: I think that the Greek view of society as static has to follow from their value system being based in that kind of thinking.

HJM: It follows from their philosophical assumptions that this is a well-ordered, rational universe in which each individual has his telos. He has a task to perform that is predestined, and no problem as to the station arises or as to the function to be performed. The only question is how you perform those functions most completely, most thoroughly.

Student: If society weren't static, if the station a person is born into wasn't his fixed station, then how would he know what his telos was? I mean, it could be a different telos at different points in life. And he'd be left without a telos. It has to be static.

HJM: It has to be static because otherwise the individual would be at sea. He wouldn't know what to do, since there is no substitute for the telos in some kind of dynamic principle of self-fulfillment.

Student: How would Aristotle have voted if he had returned to the Nuremberg trial? If the defendants were good citizens?[5]

HJM: Aristotle had no conception of a supranational principle of justice that one state could apply to another state, which is in itself an extraordinary legal situation. So, certainly, Aristotle would have judged the Hitler regime as a tyrannical regime. But it never occurred to him that another state (or a group of states, not possessed of complete virtue either) could sit in judgment over the delinquent state. Furthermore, they could sit in judgment only because they had defeated the delinquent state. So this is a very tenuous situation, morally and legally. I am fully aware of the popularity of the principles of Nuremberg that have been applied only once under extraordinary circumstances and are not likely to be applied again except when a victorious nation or group of nations can apply them against a defeated nation. Certainly if North Vietnam would be able to defeat the United States and capture the president of the United States, the secretary of state, a succession of members of the joint chiefs of staff, they probably would put them on trial and hang them. But it is not likely to happen.

---

5. This short section is drawn from the seminar of February 8, 1972. I have included it primarily because the students force Morgenthau to consider how the Aristotelian position would relate to war crimes, focusing on Nuremburg and Tokyo. This digression, actually discouraged by Morgenthau, provides some important insights into Morgenthau's thoughts on these issues.

The question of right in the Nuremberg case is that of might. Otherwise no one can judge the powerful. In the case of General Yamamoto, if he were guilty . . .

Student: Isn't there an analogy with something Aristotle would recognize if a tyrant is overthrown, then the revolutionary tribunal would sit in judgment upon others . . .

HJM: Yes, but you are dealing here with the same state, with a domestic situation. It is not one state who judges another state. Surely if you had a civil war, the loser or the revolutionary who loses would be put on trial for high treason, but that doesn't create any problem.

Student: What I am saying is, putting the former legitimate power on trial for treason in the name of that new power that has seized power.

HJM: Here you have the core of the statement that "might makes right," which happens to be true. If you are defeated, your crimes may be brought home to you. If you are victorious, nobody is going to judge you—not in this world. Because nobody has the power to judge you. We captured General Yamamoto[6] and put him on trial because he didn't control his troops even though he was hundreds of miles away from what happened in the Philippines. I remember I opposed the death sentence against General Yamamoto and I had some interesting correspondence with the two Supreme Court Judges, Murphy[7] and Rutledge,[8] who voted against it. I thought it was simply vengeance. And again I raise the obvious questions: If Yamamoto, who was hundreds of miles away—who physically was incapable of controlling his troops—was guilty of a violation of the law of war that earned him the death penalty, then what about what we have been doing in Vietnam? You have a situation that now is much more clearly simply the application of vengeance by the victor over the vanquished.

Student: Is it really a question of crimes against humanity?

HJM: No, certainly not. The concept of humanity is a Christian concept. You cannot even say a Judeo-Christian one; it is a Christian concept. A great step forward, a revolutionary step that Christianity made, by which it destroyed morally the ancient world, was exactly to establish an equality of all men regardless of their station in life. Not according to functions, but as the religious statement—as the children of God. This is completely alien to Aristotle.

Student: In Aristotle's perspective, a citizen of Athens might at some time have the right to kill a slave whereas the slave would not have the right to kill a citizen.

HJM: Well, that depends. Your statement empirically is certainly correct. But under what circumstances this is true depends upon the functions both performed.

---

6. This reference is unclear. My suspicion is that the transcriber incorrectly wrote down the name Morgenthau mentioned here. Admiral Isoruku Yamamoto (1884–1943) was responsible for the attack on Pearl Harbor, but he died in the midst of the war. One of the seven Japanese "A" criminals executed after the Tokyo Trials was General Heitaro Kimura, who was accused of atrocities in building a railway in the Philippines. This person is perhaps the one to whom Morgenthau refers.
7. Associate Justice Frank Murphy, who served from 1941 to 1949.
8. Associate Justice Wiley Blount Rutledge, who served from 1943 to 1949.

Certainly a slave who doesn't perform his functions is subject to the punishment unto death. However, let's not go into this in detail because it gets us away from Aristotle.

Student:[9] Can we equate what is happening in Vietnam with what happened to the Indians? The thing that they have in common is something that might be called genocide. There is an element of genocide in massive bombing.

HJM: For my own personal point of view, I would agree with you, but there are people who are profoundly convinced that we are performing a moral mission in Vietnam. I give you the example of a discussion I had with the man who was Vice President of the United States in 1966. I never found a man more profoundly convinced, more honestly convinced, more passionately convinced that we are engaged in a moral crusade in Vietnam.

You see surely from our point of view, from my point of view and from your point of view, what we are doing in Vietnam is a moral outrage. But for the air force generals or even for an army general whom I saw on TV the other day, Hollingsworth it was, he said that is a great thing we are killing crooks.[10] Here we are saving the world from communism and from the yellow peril. Is it not moral to defend white, Christian civilization against the yellow peril? So I see Pascal made the point about this kind of morality. He said, "If I kill you on this side of the river, I am an assassin; if I kill you on the other side of the river, I am a hero." That is the essential ambivalence of political moral judgment.

Take the Nazi genocide. From my point of view, having a personal interest in the matter, it is a moral outrage. From the point of view of a Nazi who honestly believes that the lower races are about to corrupt and destroy mankind, it is a noble deed to save mankind by getting rid of the vermin that look like human beings but really aren't. And if he believes this, as pioneers believed about the Indians, then to kill them may not only be justified but it is a noble deed. I have seen eyewitness reports from the Jacksonian period reporting how they shot Indians and describing how one Indian hit by a bullet jumped up then fell down like an animal. I mean, it was the exact same type of glee and aesthetic joy as hunters have when they kill deer or rabbits. In other words, the moral universe in which you operate depends upon your basic worldview; once you have decided what in your view the world is like, certain moral judgments follow with inevitability. This is really the burden in Hannah Arendt's analysis of Eichmann.[11] He was no monster; he was a bureaucrat who believed in certain basic values and put them into practice.

Nobody knows with absolute certainty what absolute justice requires in a particular situation. Which is exactly the Aristotelian point of view. I have convictions

---

9. This section is from the latter half of the seminar of April 11, 1972, where student questions turn Morgenthau to a discussion of ethics and politics.

10. Lt. General James F. Hollingsworth, (1918–   ) served in Vietnam and later commanded the U.S. forces in South Korea.

11. Hannah Arendt, *Eichmann in Jerusalem*, rev. ed. (New York: Penguin Books, 1994).

about what justice requires and I have convictions about the objective validity of my convictions. But since I am not a party to the councils of providence, I can only make judgments with a limited outlook and with a particular perspective and a particular set of interests that is part of my perspective. I can only hope that I approximate objective and absolute justice. But I can't be sure that I do. Certainly my view of justice is a partial view of justice and I will defend it because my own perspectives, my own interests are intimately involved in it.

You can be a fanatic and believe that you are the mouthpiece of providence, that you have all the justice there is, that the other side has none. Certain religious fanatics are, of course, the classic example of this as well as political fanatics who will kill and torture and do atrocious things because they are convinced that they have all the justice there is. A man whom I would regard to be decent and wiser will know that the best they can do is to approximate justice with the injunction of continuous error. That is as far as you can go.

How do you fill these abstract concepts of morality with concrete content? Consider Aristotle's principle of equality—to treat equal what is equal. But what is equal? What are the relevant distinctions? Men are different from women; is that a relevant distinction that has political consequences? Or is it irrelevant? From most of recorded history, it was regarded to be relevant, extremely relevant. Today it is regarded as utterly irrelevant. I am not going to stick my neck out and go any further than that. But here you have an example of the uncertainty as to what concretely is meant by a necessarily abstract principle of justice.

Consider the pragmatism of Richard Nixon. Because Mr. Nixon is a pragmatist, he can do something that nobody on the American political scene would have been able to do—he can go to Peking and offer it as a great positive thing. Nixon is a good example of a pragmatist, someone who is a completely nonideological operator. He is capable of anything; he is capable of egregious violations of moral principles, but he is also capable of pragmatic amelioration if it fits into his pragmatic scheme. The religious or pseudo-religious fanatic is capable only of trying to realize his absolute conception of justice. Which in my view is a much more dangerous kind of thing because he hasn't got any way out; he can only go ahead and destroy and kill in order to bring about the kingdom of God.

What you believe about the world is what determines your judgment and your action. Take Vietnam: If you believe that communism is a world-wide conspiracy that has to be resisted wherever it raises its ugly head because of its ubiquitous conspiratorial nature, certain moral judgments and certain political actions follow from that basic assumption. If you want an explanation of our continuous involvement in Vietnam, under three entirely different presidents, the answer is all three presidents operated within a worldview that made the resistance to communism in Vietnam a vital concern of the United States.

Do moral principles change in politics? There have certainly been changes in morally and legally relevant behavior. Take, for instance, the immunity of diplomatic representatives. There were long periods of history when it was perfectly permissible and an accepted practice of princes and states to try to kill (especially to poison) obnoxious statesmen and diplomats. The republic of Venice had an official poisoner—a civil service position, you may say. We have the records, the diaries of those people who wrote down, "We used so much arsenic and so much such and such and he died after two days of convulsions." We have the records of one poisoner of the republic of Venice who tried his luck six times on the Emperor Maximilian, without any success; either he was incompetent or the emperor had a particularly strong constitution. And this was generally accepted. We have records of a papal coronation dinner in the sixteenth century to which the cardinals came with their own cooks because they wanted to come out alive. Everybody took it for granted that you can poison your opponent. But one thing wasn't done and that was to poison wells. This was regarded as unfair practice. It was immoral. Of course, all this is absolutely relative, and it is obvious that certain things are allowed under certain historic conditions or in certain societies and others are not.

Take the strict distinction that was made in the nineteenth and beginning of the twentieth century between combatants and civilians—or military personnel able and willing to fight and military personnel wounded or willing to surrender. The distinction was strictly made and observed. And when, for instance, some civilians in the war of 1870 fought against the Germans, there was an outcry against this unfair practice. And when the German armies in the First World War executed some Belgians and French civilians, there was also an outcry. And there was an outcry when the Germans bombed Warsaw, Coventry, and Rotterdam at the beginning of the Second World War. At the end of the Second World War the bombings of Hamburg and Nuremberg and Cologne and Munich and Hiroshima and Nagasaki were taken for granted. So I am not really raising the question as to what is responsible for those changes—technology or a decay of moral values—but the radical changes are obvious. Look at Vietnam today.

Student: Moore[12] said: "The good is not definable." Good cannot be defined.

HJM: Moore belongs to a particular philosophic school that tries to eliminate philosophy by semantics—by showing the semantic impossibility of complete and objective definition. I think justice or the good can be defined, but the definition is bound to be empty and abstract. And has to be filled with historic content. Here the problems and difficulties arise.

---

12. G.E. Moore (1873–1958) was a British moral philosopher who helped create modern analytic philosophy. Morganthau's critique of him refers to the analytic method of focusing on the meaning of words as the proper mode of philosophy—a distinct difference from Aristotle.

CHAPTER 5

Power, Interests, and the Common Good

In Book 3, Chapter 6, Aristotle states the following: "Having determined this question, we have next to consider whether there is only one form of government or many, and if many, what they are and how many, and what are the differences between them."[1]

This is, of course, the famous division among monarchy, aristocracy, and constitutional government, and its perversions, tyranny, oligarchy, and democracy. The first observation one has to make concerns the term constitution, which in Aristotle doesn't mean a written document, a legally binding organization of the state, but rather the actual distribution of power. It is very much like what we would call a living constitution. Or what the German socialist leader LaSalle referred to when he gave a couple of lectures in the 1860s with the title, "What Is

---

In the following section, Morgenthau turns to Aristotle's division of governments found in Book 3, Chapters 6–13. Morgenthau uses this section of Aristotle to explore the idea of interests and power as they relate to governance. His interpretation of this material does not appear to have changed from his first set of recorded lectures on Aristotle, which took place in 1947. One student's lecture notes from that series, found in Morgenthau's papers, states the following: "While Aristotle's initial distinction among the different types of government is numerical, i.e., whether it is one, the few, or the many, he goes on to say that this is only an incidental attribute of the essential distinction which is wealth. . . . The relationship between numbers and wealth is incidental and usual, but is not a necessary relationship, according to Aristotle. . . . Morgenthau, on the contrary, feels that there is a necessary relationship between wealth and numbers since wealth is not only an economic concept but a social concept." From "Notes on Lectures by Professor H. J. Morgenthau," Winter Quarter 1947, Morgenthau Papers, Box 76, Library of Congress, Washington DC.

1. 1278b5-10. This quote suggests that Morgenthau used the Benjamin Jowett translation of *The Politics*, reprinted in Richard McKeon's *The Basic Works of Aristotle* (New York: Random House, 1941). This is a verbatim quote found on page 1184.

a Constitution?"[2] He said, "The army, that is the constitution. The police, that is the constitution. The bankers, that is the constitution." And so forth. In other words, he described the real constitution, the real distribution of power in a state as over against its legal one. So, when we talk here about types of government, we are talking about concrete political conditions and not a legal abstraction. So if Aristotle had raised the question of the constitution of the Soviet Union, he wouldn't have meant the written document with its bill of rights and protection of citizens and so forth, but he would have meant what is actually going on in the Soviet Union in political terms. Where does the actual power reside? And if he had raised that question with regard to the United States before the Civil War, he would not have referred primarily to the constitutional arrangements, but to the actual distribution of power. And he would have said that the basic issue of any constitution of any political organization in the empirical sense is, where does the supreme power in the state lie? Where does sovereignty lie? And he would have arrived at the conclusion that this question is in abeyance.

It hasn't been decided in America where actual sovereignty lies, whether it lies with the federal government or with the states. And Aristotle might have looked at the Civil War as a means by which this constitutional question was decided in favor of the government because John Calhoun,[3] the political philosopher of the South, saw eye to eye with the Federalists in the Philadelphia Constitutional Convention, in that both were of the opinion that sovereignty couldn't be divided. That it had to be here or there, that it couldn't be in two places at the same time. And there are some striking statements in Calhoun that support what all speakers with the exception of one, Hamilton, said in the Constitutional Convention, namely, that a division of sovereignty is a contradiction in terms, even though the constitutional doctrine accepted this idea of the division of sovereignty for political reasons. But for Aristotle, this would have been an empirical question—that is, where does sovereignty lie? And he would have found that it does not lie anywhere in particular. This creates a very unhealthy and precarious situation. The Civil War decided that issue in favor of the Union because the federal government happened to have won the Civil War. If the Confederacy had won the Civil War, Calhoun would have been borne out and sovereignty wouldn't have lain in Washington but in the several capitals of the states of the Confederacy.

If the North had lost the Civil War, in all probability all states would have been sovereign and the government in Washington would have been a kind of United Nations. Lincoln was fully aware of this. Lincoln said, "We are fighting in order to preserve the Union." This is to say, a central government that is sovereign. The

---

2. Ferdinand LaSalle (1825–1864) was a Prussian socialist who knew Marx. Unlike Marx, however, LaSalle argued more directly for a version of state socialism.

3. John C. Calhoun (1782–1850) served as representative, senator, secretary of war, vice president, and senator again. He was, as Morgenthau notes, one of the most articulate defenders of the Confederacy's claim to separate from the Union.

issue was really the location of sovereignty, not only for the Confederacy but also for all concerned, for all states. And if the Union had lost the war, in all likelihood the claim to sovereignty of all the states would have been confirmed.

So, when Aristotle talks about constitutional government as the sound counterfoil to the corruption of democracy, what he is referring to is a well-ordered commonwealth in which there is an efficient and equitable distribution of power between the people at large and the government and in which the people at large do not have the ultimate power, have not sovereignty within the state. Aristotle makes this point very clear by saying, "The government is sovereign in the state and the constitution is in fact the government."[4] So we should be very careful when we read here the term "constitution" that we are not tempted to think of the term in the same way in which we talk about the Constitution of the United States. This is not what Aristotle means at all. What he means is the actual political situation in the country.

In order to develop this typology of forms of government—monarchy, aristocracy, constitutional government, the good forms of government, and their corruption, tyranny, oligarchy and democracy—Aristotle goes back to the basic issue. And that is, that man is a political animal, that in order to fulfill himself, to achieve his telos, he must live in a political community. The question then is, what does this basic fact mean in terms of the different types of government? And then he comes back to the relation between master and servant and tells us again about the common interest that the two have and that both serve the same purpose. The difference then, according to him, between good, healthy governments and corrupted governments is to what extent they meet the requirement of governing on behalf of the common interest. That is to say, we have again here this kind of organic, teleological conception of man and society, that man has a purpose, has a telos that he cannot achieve by his own efforts. He has to enter into political ties with other similarly situated individuals. He is not self-sufficient, and in order to achieve his telos he must cooperate in a political way with other individuals. He can cooperate with them in different ways, but there is one basic distinction insofar as the cooperation serves the common ends of all, that is to say, to achieve their telos. Those governments are sound, are good, and are healthy governments. Insofar as they serve the purposes, the interests of certain special groups within the political commonwealth, they are bad, corrupted governments. So it follows, of course, that in empirical terms, all governments are corrupted because no government serves the common purpose without qualification, without taking into account the interests of the rulers. And so the real practical question is, which is the form of government that minimizes the use of government for selfish purposes and not for the common interest.

Of course, there is one basic issue that Aristotle doesn't consider and that in all probability he cannot afford to consider for philosophic, if not for practical

---

4. 1278b-10. From Aristotle, *The Politics*, another direct quote from McKeon, *The Basic Works of Aristotle*, p. 1184.

political reasons. That is, how do you define the common interest? What is the common good, the *bonum commune* that medieval philosophers such as Thomas Aquinas elaborated? For Aquinas and Aristotle, the common good is self-evident. It is the cooperation of all concerned on behalf of their achievement of their respective teloi. But this is, of course, for us an open question. If we just refer to the headlines of this morning, is the SST in the common interest?[5] Is the family support plan in the common interest? Are the new weapons system long-range submarine based missiles on the bottom of the ocean in the public interest? Who is going to decide what is in the public interest? Evidently, in a democracy either the executive or the majority of the legislature will decide what is in the common interest. In a monarchy the king will decide. In an aristocracy the aristocracy will decide. But who subjects the decisions of the majority, of the king, or of the aristocracy to the transcendent scrutiny? Because somebody says this is in the public interest, it doesn't follow that it actually is. This issue Aristotle doesn't and cannot see at all.

The other alternative to justify the majority will as the expression of the public interest is that there is an inherent virtue, an inherent wisdom in the people at large so that when the people at large have spoken, the public interest has been revealed. *Vox populi, vox dei.* This is again a philosophy that is open to certain doubt by virtue of our experiences with totalitarianism. A totalitarian regime generally governs with the support and sometimes with the enthusiastic support of the majority of the people. If you look at Nazism in Germany, there can't be any doubt, or at least there isn't any doubt in my mind, that there has never been a government in Germany that had more genuine and more enthusiastic and more widespread support among the people at large. In a sense, this was a genuinely democratic government. If you limit the adjective of democratic to popular support, however achieved, is one then going to say that whatever the majority wants is identical with the common good? This, of course, is the conclusion Mr. Justice Holmes arrived at when he said, "I have no other criterion for the quality of a law except what the crowd wants," which is, of course, the ultimate in skepticism. We don't even pretend to have a transcendent objective criterion for the public interest. We say it is the public interest because the crowd wants it.

This is a very crucial issue for modern political philosophy because if you assume that there is no objective standard whatsoever, you of course eliminate also the concept of truth from political philosophy. You would have nothing but a universe where different groups struggle with each other and where justice and the common good are identical with whomever happens to prevail at a particular moment in this struggle. Or else you must find an objective platform from which you can judge what is in the public interest and what is not. While it so happens that all of us assume that such an objective platform exists, none of us when he enters

---

5. The headline apparently refers to the agreement between France and England to produce the first supersonic commercial airline, known as the SST. As a result, transcontinental flight was reduced from 7–8 hours to approximately 4 hours.

the political arena assumes that it is really nothing more than a struggle between different pressure groups, each of which has the same right or the same moral dignity in representing the public interest. We assume without any question that certain interests have a higher moral dignity than others. It generally happens that it is our own interests that have a higher moral dignity. But the very fact that nobody will argue in absolute terms testifies to the vitality of the concept of the common good and the public interest itself. The defenders of the oil depletion allowance try to make a point that this is in the public interest. They say it's good for us and to hell with the rest of the world. Only a naive man like Charles Wilson could say that what is good for General Motors is good for the United States.[6] No knowledgeable political operator will limit himself to such a simpleminded claim. He will say, "What we want, we don't want for only ourselves. We want it for the nation because it's good for the nation."

It still remains an open question whether it is in the public interest or not, and they will say, it is *not* in the public interest, but we can't do anything about it. Take the Vietnamese war. I happen to believe that it is not in the public interest to fight in Vietnam and I will probably say so forever after. But this does not dispose of the issue. The majority has spoken, you may say. The president has spoken, a succession of presidents have spoken, all going in this direction. I, almost alone for a while, went in the other direction. The U.S. government and I both made our cases in terms of the public interest. The issue is never settled and majority rule will not settle it. If the Congress would unanimously come out in favor of the Vietnam War, we'd still be against it. Not because of a personal stubbornness, but because I would still say it is not in the national interest. So, the point I want to make is that in spite of the obvious impossibility to prove with general persuasiveness that one policy is in the national interest and another is not, we all assume that there is an objective criterion by which we can at least approximate the truth as to what serves the public good and what does not.

Student: How would you respond to the argument there is no public interest, but that this is always used by people who want to justify themselves in positions of power.

HJM: Or out of power. Take Marxism. Marxism certainly says, "Capitalism is against the public interest." It is a rule of a minority over the majority. We are representing the public interest.

If one accepts your view, no one could fight with a good conscience, that is, if there were nothing at stake but his interests. This is the dialectic of politics within a society comprising different classes and all classes accepting membership in this society. If the Marxist prophecy of the international proletariat had come about, transcending loyalties to particular national societies, even then you wouldn't have a point because then the proletariat would fight not for its own class but for mankind. And this is what, of course, the Communists have always maintained.

---

6. Charles E. Wilson made this famous statement at his Senate confirmation hearings to become Eisenhower's secretary of defense in 1953.

There is this beautiful and revealing episode in the hearings of the Canadian Royal Commission on the Igor Gouzenko report.

Gouzenko was a Russian code clerk in the Soviet Embassy in Ottawa who defected in the late 1940s and uncovered the complete spy ring of the Soviet Union in Canada and the United States, especially with regard to atomic energy, and implicated a considerable number of high officials of Canada and Great Britain. This Royal Commission, which acted with perfect impartiality in the best tradition of British justice, asked each of the accused: "Why did you do it?" With one exception, all said, "We didn't have any monetary advantages." One got, I think, some travel allowance or whatever it was. They just asked, "Why did you do it?" and they all said, "Because we are convinced that the interests of the Soviet Union are identical with the interests of mankind and therefore take precedence over the interests of Great Britain or Canada." Nobody said, "This is in our personal interests." Or, "This is in the interests of a particular class."

You see, man happens to be a moral being who cannot operate on the basis of calculated self-interest alone. Whatever the actual function of what he is doing is, he must convince himself and others that what he is doing he does not do for himself but, to paraphrase Cavour, for Italy, for some transcendent good. Perhaps Cavour also acted in good measure for himself, for his own glory, his own ego, or what not.[7] Nobody has analyzed it, but in any event he must convince himself, and Marx must convince himself, that what he does and what he propagates is not for a parochial interest of a particular group but is for mankind. This is the liberation of mankind. This is to make an end to history itself. For this you can suffer, for this you can fight, for this you can die. For the oil depletion allowance by itself, nobody is going to go and mount the barricades and die. But if it comes to free enterprise, the American way of life, that's a different story.

Sure, most of the invocations of the public interest or the common good are hypocritical. They are untrue, objectively. But the fact that everybody feels the absolute necessity to invoke the public interest, the common good, the national interest, testifies to its objective validity even though nobody knows exactly what it is. And this is true of the national interest in foreign policy as well. No nation could say, "We want this piece of territory or that influence in a foreign nation because we want power and we want to increase the reach of our power." They all have to say, "We want it either for the common good of mankind or for the common good of Western civilization or communism or for the common good of Russia, Germany, the United States, or what not." This is always hovering above the struggles of groups of individuals. Each tries to put it over to his side. Nobody ever can, but the very urge to do this testifies to its existence.

Student: Aren't you contradicting your own theory by saying this?

HJM: Why?

---

7. Count Camillo Benso di Cavour (1810–1861) was an Italian statesman who helped create a unified Italy and served as its prime minister.

Student: Because in political realism, don't you say that intent and motive is not what is important in politics, it's the action. So just because everybody says that it's usually not true, to justify their own power actions for themselves, how can you say that the common interest really exists.

HJM: Of course you can't really say that it exists, but what you can say is that one cannot think about political matters without taking the assumption of its existence into account because this is the framework, that is, the frame of reference with which the political discussion and political action operates.

Student: You said that the person who is using the common interest has to convince himself and others that what he is doing is in the common interest. For example, the generals in the Pentagon are convinced that the war in Vietnam is in the national interest. But for people who have to fight this war, it's completely opposite to their interest.

HJM: No, it is not completely opposite. If you talk about Vietnam, the armed forces are divided as the people at large are divided. The members of the armed forces who regard the war as not in the national interest or even a moral outrage is certainly in the minority. But this is neither here nor there. In other words, there isn't any consensus of opinion in the armed forces about this, and even if there were, it wouldn't make any difference. But the point I'm making is that the compulsion for all concerned to justify their position within the political arena and their political actions in terms of an objective factor transcending their parochial interests is in itself an objective political fact that one has to take into account.

Student: What you are talking about is recognition of a technique for success. If I were a politician, I would realize that I must say certain things in order to be elected. The Pentagon must say similar things, use its cunning to trick people into thinking it's in their interest.

HJM: But they believe it. They are not so cunning, they may be cunning, too, but they don't mouth convictions that they don't have themselves. They are actually convinced that the more nuclear and the better nuclear weapons you have, the better off you are. What one should not underestimate is the ability of man for self-deception and for pigheadedness. I have just read a little book by Professor Graff on the operation of the so-called Tuesday Cabinet[8]—that is to say, the few people who had lunch with President Johnson and at which the political decisions were made. If you read those verbatim accounts, especially of what Mr. Johnson said, it is truly frightening. That's the way we are governed. I'm writing something on this, so I don't need to give you a preview here; otherwise you won't read it![9] Don't underestimate the lack of information, the plain stupidity of policymakers. So the idea that they are cunning, I think, gives them frequently much too much credit. They believe what they say, however unbelievable that may sound.

---

8. Henry F. Graff, *The Tuesday Cabinet: Deliberation and Decision on Peace and War under Lyndon B. Johnson* (Englewood Cliffs, NJ: Prentice Hall, 1970).

9. I am not sure to which of his own writings Morgenthau refers here.

Student: You say that this shows that people are seeking the validity of an objective factor, but it would seem to me that the objective factor is that people have a psychological need for some reference point outside themselves that would satisfy the objective fact.

HJM: Well, strike out objective factor. I myself felt when I said it that it wasn't right. But what you have is certainly almost psychological. But then you have to ask yourself, "Where does the psychological compulsion come from?" Why is it, in other words, that the individual cannot be satisfied with defending and promoting his own personal interests or what he thinks his own personal interests are without relating those interests to an objective transcendent factor that we call the national interest? This is in itself a fact that requires explanation, which you cannot dismiss or devaluate by saying it is psychological. But why is it a part of the psychology of all man?

Student: I agree with you. I think there is a moral end. I think this is one of the problems, that people underestimate this moral factor and the very individualistic and psychological Freudian aspect involved. But the only thing that I'm questioning is whether man needs other men to the extent that he has to say, "What I'm doing is really for the good of all men." Maybe once the revolutionaries take power and this has always been true, they say, "We rule in the interest of all the people." And sometimes they say, "No, we're only interested in the workers who happen to be the majority."

HJM: O.K., but which then replaces all the people. Then the majority becomes the empirical expression of the interests of all the people. That is, of course, true in democracy. Since you can't have unanimity in order to express the will of the people, majority is the next best thing. It is the next approximation to the *volunte general*, the general will.

Student: Does that mean that the limits of creating a democratic or a just society, of creating a common interest lie in what the executive or the ruler or rulers determine to be the common interest? In other words, his subjective interpretation of the common interest is the criterion by which the common good is observed?

HJM: This is true to a very great extent throughout history. Again to use the Marxist term, the consciousness of man is determined by the ruling minority that determines what the national interest is. And for long periods of history, people have followed the Aristotelian pattern and have been satisfied with the position within the political commonwealth that the ruling group assigned to them, saying, "This is in the national interest. You perform the role of the toenails in the human body and we perform the role of the brains or of the heart. You are not very important, but we are essential." Surely, but this is exactly the point I have made before, that the Aristotelian scheme is a perfect instrument for the preservation of the status quo and for the legitimization of the status quo, and has been mostly used for that purpose. Look at the whole medieval Catholic philosophy, the organic conception of the state, which says the position you take has not been imposed upon you arbitrarily but is the expression of the objective nature of things.

Surely, you are entirely correct, but then you have the countertendency, which is of modern origin, to question this static conception of society and to submit it to some other presumably objective tests. Then you get a dynamism in which especially the submerged classes question the naturalness and the justness of the status quo and use different criteria to determine what is in their interest and what is in the common interest.

The point I'm making is that there is still a reference to an objective factor by which political events are judged, and that it is not a matter of mere struggles between pressure groups or between parochial interest groups, but is also a struggle between different moral conceptions as to what the state ought to be and what the position of certain individuals within the state ought to be. In other words, politics is not only a struggle for power, it is also a moral struggle for the preservation or the extension or the victory of certain moral values. And this is what the whole concept of the national interest, or the common good, or the public interest is all about.

Two weeks ago we started to discuss one of the great contributions of Aristotle to philosophy, the distinction of different types of government—the good government and the perverted government.[10] As you will remember, the distinction is based on the difference between different types of government regardless of whether they are good or bad, whether it is a government of one man, the government of the few, or the government of the many. Then the distinction is made among the good government of one man, which is a monarchy; the government of the few, which is also good, the aristocracy; and the government of the many, which is the constitutional government; and the perverted types that correspond to the one, few, and many, which are tyranny, oligarchy, and democracy. The question, of course, arises, how to distinguish between a good and a bad government. What is the distinction that Aristotle makes?

For Aristotle, the distinction depends on the idea of the common good. That is really the distinction that divides the three good from the three bad types of government. A monarch is supposed to govern for the good of all, for the public interest; the aristocracy and the constitutional government do the same. The tyrant works only for himself or for a small group of people, in any case, not for the common good. The same is true for the oligarchy and for the democracy. Furthermore, there is a distinction between the aristocracy and the oligarchy on the one hand and the constitutional and the democratic forms of government on the other, and that is that the aristocracy and the oligarchy are governments of the wealthy. The difference is that the aristocrats govern for the common good while the oligarchs govern for themselves, or for a group, for a class, let me say. In the same

---

10. A seminar from December 18, 1970, begins here. As I noted earlier, the interpretation Morgenthau has of Aristotle here remains true to his 1948 lecture notes—taking the division of government as a qualitative one and not simply about the number of rulers by drawing on a vague notion of social position.

way, in the constitutional government the many govern for the whole, for the public interest; and democracy governs for the sake of the poor because it is a government of the poor.

Aristotle then raises at least a theoretically legitimate question: "What is going to happen if the majority are wealthy?" If you have what we would call today a middle-class society where there are no really poor, would this be an aristocracy? Or would that be a constitutional government? In other words, you have a problem when you distinguish forms of government on economic grounds and identify the government of the few with the government of the wealthy because in theory you can imagine a situation in which the wealthy are the majority and the poor are the minority. Now, if the poor govern in such a situation, do we have to speak of aristocracy? Can there be an aristocracy of the poor that govern the majority of the wealthy? Or if the wealthy govern in a democracy or in a constitutional government, can we say that the poor, a minority, are governed by the majority of the wealthy? In other words, you've got a mess in the terminological sense if you equate the government of the few with the government of the wealthy and the government of the many with the government of the poor because theoretically it could be the other way around.

Of course, the distinction is superficial. It is merely quantitative: one, a few, many. Aristotle notices this, and he fills out the emptiness of the quantitative distinction by saying that the few are the wealthy and the many are the poor, which is generally the case. But logically this need not be the case. And Aristotle gets around this difficulty by saying a situation in which the majority are wealthy and the minority are poor is extraordinary, so extraordinary that in terms of terminology you don't need to consider it. Even if you don't consider for a moment the large mass of the poor even in an affluent democracy such as ours, it is still true that there is an enormous quantitative and qualitative distinction between the affluent construction worker and the Rockefellers. Even though the construction worker looks like a rich man compared with a landless peasant in Pakistan or with the conditions of industrial workers 50 or 60 years ago, he's still relatively poor as compared with the aristocracy of wealth in the country. So even if one makes allowances for changes in the wide spread of a certain degree of prosperity and affluence, it still remains a fact that there is a basic distinction between the rich and the not-so-rich that is reflected in the political situation.

You have only to consider today the economic requirements for running for public office. If you are not wealthy, or if you don't have the support of wealthy men, you can't run for office. You have only to look at the primaries in the state of New York for the last election. How many candidates, men like Mr. Nickerson, for instance, dropped out saying, "I haven't got the money. I haven't got it myself and I haven't got a sufficient number of wealthy supporters to allow me to run."[11] So

---

11. Eugene H. Nickerson (1918–2002), a Democrat active in New York politics, was appointed to the federal judiciary in 1977 by President Jimmy Carter. I have been unable to determine which year he ran for governor, or if he even considered it.

regardless of the spread of a certain degree of affluence, the basic economic distinctions that are reflected in politics still remain. It is really inconsequential in political terms that what were once called the poor are now called the lower middle class because the spread in wealth, which has political consequences, remains. Recently a foreign potentate wanted to see some poor quarters in New York. He looked and was amazed, and he said, "Well, in our country, this would be far above the level of poverty." That is, people at least live in houses or in slums. I have seen what is called the slums in Pakistan or India or certain Latin American countries, which are simply hovels, which you have perhaps to a certain degree and, I would guess, to a diminishing degree in the South but which are unknown in metropolitan centers.

What is the criterion for who rules? Is this a government of the people, by the people, and for the people? You have a universal franchise and the people, if they want to, can exercise that franchise every two, four, or six years, as the case may be, and elect the people who rule them. Now, none of us here governs, but what we can do in a democracy or in a constitutional government and what you cannot do in a monarchy, a tyranny, an aristocracy, and an oligarchy is this: You cannot get rid of your rulers and substitute them for others. This ability of the electorate, of the people at large, of the many has, of course, a direct influence upon the way we are governed because the men who govern us, generally, except for the president in his second term, want to be reelected. And in order to be reelected, you have at least to give the appearance that you rule in accordance with the preferences of the many, and the public-opinion polls have become the quantitative measurement as to what the many want, or what they are willing to tolerate; how far the government can go in governing, where the outer limits of its government are, and furthermore, what it must do in positive terms to please the many who can vote them out of office. So you have a much more complex and subtle relationship between government and the governed than is indicated by Lincoln's phrase or that is indicated by this classification.

This leads us to American domestic politics. Certainly, regardless of which party has been in power, what program has been put into the legislative hopper and has been passed, the distribution of the social power has been constant over the whole range of American history, or at least since the Civil War. You can even go farther back if you look at the South by itself. The hold that the feudal minority has had on the South has been dented, but it has remained essentially intact. If you look at the representatives of the South in Congress, the men who wield real power, the people who have been reelected and are bound to be reelected time and again because of the feudal structure of their constituencies and who, therefore, have gained seniority and with this seniority gained the virtually permanent chairmanships of key committees, which hold the actual legislative power, this is certainly one factor. The other factor is that the concentrations of wealth, of economic power have remained intact. It is true that the economic and social power of the unions has been added to them, but once it has been added to them to a great extent it works hand in glove in the political field—at least with the traditional concentrations of economic wealth. What has happened is that the modalities of that rule have been changed and that improvements of certain changes (let me use a new term) have been made in the exercise of that power, but the center of that power, the core of that power, has remained intact from the Progressive Movement through the New Deal, the New Frontier, the Great Society, and so forth. This is, I think, a striking aspect of American political life that its stability thus far has been in good measure the reflection of the stability of the distribution of social, economic, and political power.

One might argue that we have an oligarchy in the United States. If you look at certain aspects of the situation, it is certainly true. Consider how the oil interests have a stranglehold on certain legislators in the Congress. Consider the depletion allowance, which is nothing more or less than the freeing of the oil interest from the tax burden and the shifting of that tax burden to the population at large that hasn't got any remedy such as a depletion allowance.[12] Or consider the granting of oil leases both on land and in the ocean, which is again a granting of economic bounty to very special interests. And this is true of many other economic interests. Take unions, for instance, take public utilities, take the defense industry, which have the ability to influence legislation and, more particularly, administrative and executive action in their own favor. Of course, they also argue that the legislation and administrative actions that appear to favor a particular special interest actually favor the common good because the special interest happens to be identical with the common good. The oil interests have, of course, made the same point— that it provides self-sufficiency in this vital source of power to the United States. It makes the United States independent of imports and for this reason that favorable legislation, those favorable administrative and executive decisions are really not only in the interest of special interest but in the interest of the nation as a whole.

Some argue that the American system of government consists of a plurality of pressure groups that cancel each other out, what Galbraith has called the system of counter chaos.[13] It is certainly true that the government of the United States is in good measure a government that is created by pressure groups or is determined by pressure groups, but not all interests are equally represented in Washington. You and I have certain interests that are not represented in Washington. For example, the self-perpetuating military-industrial complex leads to an absolute absurdity in terms of American priorities. The self-perpetuating arms technology forces us to create ever newer weapons, ever more sophisticated and different weapons for no good reason but simply because there exists the technological possibility of creating them. The rational position—which, for instance, Louis

---

12. A depletion allowance is a deduction from income tax for a mineral resource that will eventually be exhausted, such as oil. I am unaware of the particular debates that were occurring at the time of this seminar concerning a depletion allowance for oil companies.

13. John Kenneth Galbraith, (1908–   ), who made this point in his 1958 book, *The Affluent Society* (Boston: Houghton Mifflin Co.).

Mumford recently explained in a book, and has explained in many books before—tries to put some rational direction into the technological process that now tends to overwhelm any other interests, this interest is not represented in Washington at all.[14] You have members of Congress who want to put a stop to it but the pressure groups that are potent and that have power are on the other side of the fence. By power I come back to what I've said before, that is, the financial support you can expect or your opponent can expect in the next primary or in the next election. Because a potent argument that is made time and again in Washington is, "If you don't vote for this, we are going to put up a rival to you in the next primaries and we will give him a million dollars to beat you." This is a very powerful argument if you've got only $50,000 and if you didn't have a potent opponent in the last primary. To ruin you, to get you out of political life by running a candidate in the primary against you, is a very potent argument. And if you are not absolutely sure of your reelection or renomination, and few people outside the South can be sure of this, you think twice before you meet such a powerful pressure group head-on. This is true not only of the corporations; it is true of the labor unions, too. The labor unions will tell a candidate, "If you vote for this act of Congress, we're going to drive you out of political life and we're going to run somebody against you in the primaries and in the election and we've got a kitty for the next election that you can't even begin to match."

Sometimes there is collusion among these interest groups. It is not as though one pressure group attacks here, the other pressure group attacks there, and then you have a kind of balance of power. They cancel each other out. It is really like—if I may use a somewhat disreputable simile, but the only one that comes to mind right now—it's like a pack of rats. They attack the pie from different directions and each gets a part of the pie. But the large group of people who are not so organized, and more particularly who have no such social and economic power, they are not in the game. They don't participate even in this kind of nibbling at the pie. Or, you may say, like a school of sharks. They don't compete with each other when they find a body in the water. Each pulls out a piece of the corpse. This is what you have here. But the people at large are either not represented at all or they are underrepresented. There are certain groups of independent citizens who try to counteract this near monopoly of certain pressure groups. Take the Council for a Livable World, which was founded by Leo Szilard, one of the originators of nuclear fission, and which collects every year a considerable amount of money to give to candidates (either in the primaries or in the election) who have committed themselves to certain programs, especially with regard to technology, disarmament, and so forth.[15] One might also

---

14. Lewis Mumford (1895–1990) was a social critic, architect, and philosopher who became famous with the publication of *Technics and Civilization* in 1934 (New York: Harcourt, Brace and Co.). Morgenthau may be referring to *The Myth in the Machine*, which was published in 1970 (New York: Harcourt, Brace and Co.).

15. Leo Szilard (1898–1964) was a Hungarian immigrant who, along with Albert Einstein, helped the United States create the atomic bomb. Morgenthau is referring to his work after the war in which he was actively engaged in nuclear disarmament and arms control.

consider the Committee for an Effective Congress, which supports on a bipartisan basis those whom it regards to be the best candidate both in the primaries and in the election, and also collects a considerable amount of money with which it counteracts, and not without a certain measure of success, the kind of economic threat to political independence that certain economic interests are able to apply.[16] So there are attempts, and not unsuccessful attempts. I wouldn't say they are all over successful but they have, in the large elections, for instance, had a considerable effect upon the election of certain candidates who were in marginal situations and who won against the organized attempts of powerful economic interests to defeat them. Still, if you look at the overall picture, it is certainly true that any candidate who embraces a position that violates the interests of one of those groups will have a difficult time getting elected. Take the media, which are also important and which can greatly diminish the influence of an individual candidate, if not by virtually canceling him out. If they don't give him equal access to newspapers, radio, television, or if they consistently misrepresent his views, here the power of the mass media in a negative sense is enormous by simply not providing a complete spectrum of political opinion.

Student: I would argue that there is no public interest as far as I'm concerned. The other thing that I would argue is that the basic division is class. In America, the difference between middle class and working class is still a viable distinction even though it is not used. Also, there is competition within classes, and all the groups that you've mentioned happen to be middle class and we're all competing for that piece of the pie. Further, the Committee for an Effective Congress just wants another piece of that pie. But if you pull out and take a broader look at the areas not represented directly on your diagram there—

HJM: Don't call it a diagram.

Student: Well, the circles.

HJM: Futuristic abstract drawing.[17]

Student: Anyway, you say there are groups nowhere near the pie. I think that's what you have to look at and that's the division you have to make, not the difference in the class groups but the difference between middle class and working class and that's what I would say to these students, because essentially the students are all middle class and they're fed up. They can't get near the pie. The only other point I want to make is whether in America the theoretical conceptual problems we're having is that we all assume the goodness of the pie. We've all assumed that the end of our political actions should be somehow to get that pie so

---

16. The National Committee for an Effective Congress still exists today. Its Web site lists its primary goal as helping to elect "progressive" candidates to the U.S. Congress (www.ncec.org). Morgenthau is listed as a previous member of their board of trustees. Morgenthau's description of them as bipartisan may have been true in 1970, although it does not seem likely in 2004.

17. While there is no picture of the visual representation in the lecture notes, I left this exchange in because it may suggest, if ever so mildly, Morgenthau's aversion to social scientific forms of representation and his preference for more humanist modes.

that in terms of the revolutionary movement, the black revolutionary movement or the Indian revolutionary movement, everybody is trying to organize him or herself so that they can squeeze into the pie. Well, maybe the answer is to challenge all concepts of middle-class identity and middle-class ways of living and revert not back to a commune, which is simply a perversion of middle-class living, but to the concept of solidarity and the kinds of ideals that supposedly came out of the humanistic side of socialism and working-class movement.

HJM: First of all there are probably conflicts of interest between the working class and the middle class, but they are not of an acute political nature at present. There are also conflicts of interest between instructors and assistant professors that are not of an acute political nature. There are all kinds of conflicts of interest. There are conflicts of interest between husbands and wives, for instance. If you are married, you are aware of this. But the real conflict that you have in the United States is not a conflict of class in the traditional Marxist or sociological sense. First of all, there is the conflict of race, where you have a whole group of people in the United States of which neither the middle-class nor the working-class philosophy and ideology in political action has taken any account until recently. Even today, it takes them into account only in a kind of ritualistic, sentimental sense. If you want to take a realistic account of the problem of race in the United States, you have to curtail perhaps not the economic interests but the social status of certain groups in American society. In other words, there isn't a blank spot, there isn't an empty room, you may say, which is reserved for the submerged races and we only need take a key and open the door and let them come in. If you let them come in, you are bound to violate what other groups, especially the working class and the lower middle classes and even the upper middle classes regard as their vested interests. Take the question of housing, which is a real emotional and economic interest of those groups, of the great majority of the American people who have a stake in society. Those who are deprived of decent housing and who want to have decent housing run up against the vested interests of other groups in American society. This has nothing to do with the traditional class divisions of which Marx and Lenin and the sociologists have spoken.

One might also consider the voiceless poor in the United States regardless of class. If you consider that according to the Bureau of the Census, 25 million Americans are poor in a technical sense, that millions are undernourished or actually hungry, this has nothing to do with class. The working class isn't interested in those people at all. They regard those people as a threat to the status they have achieved because they have moved into the lower levels of American society and have established a status. And if you look at the social history of the United States, you will always find, especially with regard to immigration, which is in a sense a question of race and religion, that the last wave that has just barely been able to establish itself in relative objective security but with enormous subjective psychological insecurity, looks down on the next wave and defends themselves against the next wave, which presses against them. So what you have always had in the nineteenth and the beginning of the twentieth century in consequence of consecutive waves of immigration, you have now internally; that those people who have arrived long ago but have been submerged and were really regarded as the objects of the political process, blacks and Indians, all of a sudden invoke the same principles on their behalf that other Americans have successfully invoked for themselves before. You cannot put this very complex and enormously important event and development, important because it threatens the very cohesion of American society, you cannot put this into the nineteenth-century framework of classes.

What the working class wants is to move into the middle class, to become indistinguishable from the middle class. You're a good Marxist because you give us all the old-fashioned arguments, for instance, about the exploitation of race conflict by the capitalistic class. Of course, the same argument we must make about anti-Semitism, about national conflicts. Take Otto Bauer who argued that in the classless society you will have no anti-Semitism, you'll have no ethnic conflicts, you will have no national conflicts because they have all been created by capitalism.[18] This goes back to Marx. In capitalism, as it were, the class division of society takes the place of original sin; in other words, all the evils in the world stem from it. I remember when I was a student at the University of Berlin that I once had a debate with a fellow student who said to me that diabetes was a capitalistic disease; it was an outgrowth of capitalism because only people who overeat, who are capitalists, get diabetes. I was not convinced then and I have not been convinced since that this is so, but this is not an important argument. The position you take is that, eliminate the classic Marxist class divisions and you will also have eliminated the racial problem that has been stimulated, aggravated, if not created, exploited at least by the capitalistic classes. Probably it has been exploited under certain conditions, but it certainly has not been created by it; and its acuity, the real danger, the real threat it constitutes if it is not solved has nothing to do with the class division of society at all. It is an existential issue that simply thrives on the physical differences between different groups of people and draws certain moral and social and political conclusions from those social differences. I'll be sure to come to this next time when we discuss the problem of equality.

You have racial problems in the Soviet Union. For instance, the blacks from Africa who study in Moscow have been discriminated against, beaten up, and so forth, because they are black. So this is an issue that far transcends the classic Marxist argument.

Student: I think you and Stokely Carmichael would get along very well.[19]

HJM: I haven't made that test yet. I shall be glad to find out.

---

18. Otto Bauer (1882–1938) was an Austrian socialist who served in the post–World War I Austrian government.

19. Stokely Carmichael (1941–1998) was a black activist who broke with the mainstream civil rights groups to join the Black Panthers. He was accused of advocating a form of black racism.

Student: One of the reasons he left the Black Panthers was because they insisted on working with white people and, really, one of the implications of your argument is that integration as a concept is ultimately not feasible.

HJM: I have not said that.

Student: Sure, you're saying that the difference between races is something existential and not rooted in economics. Perhaps there are cultural conflicts or conflicts in terms of values, and these will always exist.

HJM: I have not said that they will always exist. I only said that they are not class conflicts.

Student: I wanted to ask to what extent has this class consciousness developed into a psychological phase in that even if you obliterate the economic differences in American society today, a psychological bias has been rooted into middle class values so they have to have someone to look down upon.

HJM: That's entirely correct. You see, what no social class can really afford is to have nobody to look down upon, to be at the bottom of the social pyramid. The black anti-Semitism is to a considerable extent an expression of this as probably the racism of certain Jews is also an expression of this. But the fear, especially among blue-collar workers who have just barely established security and who can still look down on the blacks but are threatened, for instance, now by unemployment and by pricing themselves out of the labor market—those people have no class solidarity either with the white poor or with the blacks. They fear them as their main social enemy. This has nothing to do with economics per se. Economics may be an element in it but it is essentially social status, like the fear of losing your home, or of the value of your home being diluted by the intrusion of blacks into your block, that has become a fanatical obsession on the part of the blue-collar workers. In other words, the social problems we are facing are infinitely more complex than nineteenth-century liberalism or Marxism suggests.

I believe it was less complex when Marx wrote because then you really had a very simple situation. You had the proletarian who was at the mercy of the employer, and you had the employer who really exploited the proletarian. This was a simple truth and Marx translated this simple existential juxtaposition into a sophisticated social and economic theory. I remember in my early youth this was very strong. My father was a physician in Germany and I sometimes accompanied him on his calls. I remember once we went to the house of a worker who was dying of cancer and he said to my father, "When I'm dead, put this book (a kind of pamphlet) in my pocket." After we left the house, I asked my father, "What was this book that he was referring to? Was it the Bible?" My father said with a certain contempt in his voice, "That was his Bible; it was the *Communist Manifesto*." You wouldn't find this today among the members of the AFL-CIO. In other words, this was the Marxist situation. Marxism in its time was the philosophic expression of an objective existential situation. But this situation does no longer exist with regard to what we call the worker in America. It still exists with regard to the blacks and the poor whites who are unaffected by Marxism.

Student: We appear to be excluding class *and* race as explanations, whereas one side wants to argue in terms of class, the other side wants to argue in terms of race. I think if you can understand American society in terms of blacks and Chicanos and Indians, you're going to have to argue in terms of both explanations. I would agree with you that racism is an important part of understanding American society. Tocqueville talked about that as early as the 1800s. You can't totally eliminate class simply because black people constitute a class of poor people, the majority of black people.

HJM: What you say is certainly correct. There exists at least a certain measure of solidarity between a not insubstantial middle-class black population in the United States and poor blacks because of the solidarity of race; and the point I'm making is not that class is insignificant, but that you cannot put the social, political, and economic tensions that exist in the United States into the procrustean bed of class. In other words, the issue of race and the issue of social status, which is in essence a psychological or moral concept, cut across the issue of class and to a considerable extent invalidate it. In other words, the solidarity of race and the common concern for social status may overwhelm whatever there still exists within American society of the issue of class.

Student: But if you examine the history of the civil rights movement, you'll see that insofar as the black middle class made the demands, as in the fifties and early sixties, the kinds of demands that the early SNCC[20] movement made, the NAACP made, such as middle class demands of status and equality, these were easily met by the political system. As soon as the demands started to take effect in terms of welfare and economic grievances, then the system no longer seems to be accountable.

HJM: Yes, but it is not so much economic as it is social. What are the hard-hats afraid of? They may be afraid of losing their jobs, but this is very unlikely on an objective competition with a large group of people who may destroy the social status that they have just barely acquired. It really becomes a question of human contact, especially in housing patterns and so forth. And not primarily that they will lose their job—because the union rules are so elaborate, especially with regard to seniority, that there is very little chance, even if the blacks were admitted in any numbers to unions, that they would displace the present union membership. They may replace it in the long run; if the old men die out and the blacks come in, they might *replace* them, but they are not going to *displace* them.

Student: I want to get away from this. I want to talk about this classification, divisions we couldn't all agree on. Somebody like Machiavelli might argue that when you're talking about monarchies, tyrannies, and so on you're talking about the

---

20. The Student Non-Violent Coordinating Committee was an organization created by college students to coordinate nonviolent resistance to racist policies in the U.S. South in 1960. It went on to become one of the most important civil rights groups, launching the careers of many African American leaders.

same thing because there is nobody, or very, very few people who get into politics for the common good, not for self-interest. We spoke last week about the fact that everybody says that they're acting for the common good—tyrannies say the same thing; they're always arguing it. Democracies are saying the same thing, as the good forms of government. I mean, for example, some political scientists might argue that everybody is motivated by self-interest, by the drive for power.

HJM: But you see, we have not dealt with one concept that is crucial for Aristotle: the concept of justice. In other words, a government that tries to accomplish justice is different qualitatively from a government that doesn't try. Certainly there is a qualitative difference between the government of a Battista[21] or a Trujillo[22] and a government of Franklin D. Roosevelt or Eisenhower or Castro. Can you defend the proposition that the distinction between those different types, let's say, of monarchs is quantitative and not qualitative?

Student: Perhaps the differences relate to the different powers in society. Battista might have been stronger, let's say, but there weren't too many opposing him.

HJM: Yes, but why was he stronger? Because he killed everybody off who opposed him! If Roosevelt had put the Supreme Court, which invalidated his legislation, against the wall of the Supreme Court and shot them, he would have been much stronger.

Student: But he couldn't have done it . . .

HJM: He couldn't have done it. O.K., but why couldn't he have done it?

Student: Well, maybe the people wouldn't have supported him.

HJM: Why didn't the people support him? Because there was a conception of justice that put effective limits upon the power of the ruler. You may say he *had* to accept them. But, of course, he accepted them. In other words, he acted within a moral and legal framework that limited his powers to a very considerable extent. Take [Battista's] attempt to purge the Senate, which was a complete failure. Battista didn't have the problem because he shot his opponents. He had them killed. Aristotle isn't blind to the issue he has raised. He says that all governments, all rulers only embrace a partial concept of justice; that a ruler who would be dedicated to absolute, complete justice would be like a god. He would stand above mankind and wouldn't really be the subject of this political and philosophical analysis. So he is not at all blind to the fact that the monarch, the king, is not an ideal ruler who operates according to nothing but justice, who forgets about his self-interest. But he says, and I think he says something that is obvious if you get away from abstractions and look at reality. There is a difference between a monarch and a tyrant. There is a difference between, let me say, any American president you want to name and a Stalin.

Student: But it's possible to have a ruler of the Soviet Union who, as a person, could be a very fine person.

---

21. Fulgencio Battista (1901–1973) ruled Cuba as a dictator until he was overthrown by Fidel Castro in 1952.
22. Rafael Trujillo (1891–1961) ruled the Dominican Republic as a dictator from 1932 to 1961.

HJM: Sure, take Khrushchev, just as a hypothetical case. Khrushchev operated within certain limits beyond which he could have gone if he'd wanted to, but he didn't go. And take the difference between a Trujillo and a Bosch, or between a Castro and a Battista. Both types belong to the same society, ruling over the same people, and the qualitative difference, I think, is obvious. Certainly, from a moral point of view, I judge Bosch[23] higher than I do Trujillo; and certainly I do Castro higher than I do Battista. The question is, why? Is this a subjective whim of mine? Is it a question of political taste? I mean, I like people with beards better than clean-shaven dictators, or what? But certainly it is the result of a moral judgment that is not merely subjective but is based upon certain objective facts. And this is the point that Aristotle makes. Certainly, you can say that all empirical forms of government are tainted by self-interest and what Aristotle calls partial justice, which is a conception of justice that is toward the self-interest of the ruler or the ruling group. But there is an objective qualitative difference between, say, a band of robbers and a government that complies, that tries to comply, or accepts certain objective standards of justice. One doesn't need to go into history or go into abstractions. Take the difference between the government of New York and the government of the Mafia, operating within the same city limits. The Mafia is a government that has three branches, has a moral code, and operates like any other government. But there is a moral, an objective difference between this oligarchic government and the government of New York, which you might call aristocratic because it is really a group of people, party bosses, industrial and labor leaders. And again the difference is not subjective; it is not a question of degree. It's not quantitative; it's qualitative. I think, as Aristotle puts it, it is the question of what is the ultimate standard of justice, or the ultimate standard, you may say, which guides the operations of the two different types of government. The Mafia doesn't make the pretense that it serves the common good. It takes as much as it can by whatever means are safe.

We are not talking here about a national government. We're talking about a government that governs a sector of the municipality of New York. In this respect the sway of both types of government is identical. But still, within those territorial limits, the Mafia is really out to gain as much for itself as it can in terms of the economic interest of the members of the Mafia, while the government of the City of New York—other than individual members who may also be out to make a living or to gain political stature—is guided by an ultimate standard that transcends those individual, personal, subjective interests. This is a concept of justice.

Now you may say that the common good as such cannot be objectively defined, and I would agree with that. But the common good as a category in the Kantian sense, as a concept that guides you, is a psychological reality, or is a social reality that determines, in the last analysis, the actions of an illegitimate government, or the actions of a legitimate government, and that distinguishes a legitimate from an

---

23. Juan Bosch (1909–2001) served as president of the Dominican Republic for seven months in 1963. When Bosch's supporters tries to take power in 1965, the United States sent military troops to prevent a leftist victory.

illegitimate government. I think, therefore, that the Aristotelian distinctions are essentially valid. Aristotle is not oblivious to the corruption of all empirical governments and to the self-interest that corrupts their sense of justice. But he makes, I think, a valid distinction, a qualitative distinction between not degrees but different kinds of corruption. There is the corruption that is inevitable in view of human nature, the egotism of human nature; and there is another corruption that consists of the absence of a transcendent concept of justice, however corrupted this concept may become in practical application.

Student: Well, that's the whole point. I would argue that perhaps the Mafia does have a transcendental concept of justice within their government, but you might still argue that their concept of justice is qualitatively different from the concept of justice of the people of the City of New York, and at that point you might compare them. But to say that they don't have any concept of justice, I think, is not really being fair. I think even Stalin perhaps had a concept of justice, but it was so different from what we think is correct.

HJM: Let's go back to the Mafia—that is a completely empirical example. Certainly, the Mafia has a concept of justice for its own members in the sense that traitors are executed, that competitors are executed, and that the right of the stronger is applied. But it has no concept of justice with regard to the community within which it rules, and its rule certainly by far transcends the membership of the Mafia itself. Whole industries, whole commercial enterprises are controlled by the Mafia. Hundreds of thousands of people work for it. You're talking about the Mafia as a closed society, but I talk about the Mafia as a government that governs large groups of people who are not members of the Mafia. And here, then, the qualitative distinction comes in.

Student: It seems to me that in comparing, say, a monarchy with a tyranny, that Aristotle wanted to make distinctions other than the qualitative morality between the individuals, and that one should see justice not as an abstract entity but as an operational relationship between the ruler and the ruled. And when I do that, I see no qualitative difference between tyranny and monarchy except the number of persons that are injured by tyranny as opposed to that in a monarchy. Because whereas the tyrant may have his police force to actually victimize people, the structuring in a monarchy may be such or in a constitutional government may be such—for instance, the way you have it in America, with various special interests, say the defense industry and so on—that they act as the force within tyranny. They prevent the good of society from reaching the people who are not actively participating in Washington to influence legislation. It seems to me that the people suffer both in a tyranny and in constitutional government, only by different routes. Therefore, the difference is quantitative and not qualitative. Even if, for instance, Nixon or any American president may be a better president than, say, Franco, the numbers in America that suffer may be more than that in Spain.

HJM: I would not argue in terms of the number of people that suffer. It is not a question of the number of people who suffer, but it is first of all a question, fundamentally, of the methods by which they are made to suffer. There is a difference between the secret police knocking at your door at three o'clock in the morning, taking you away and never to be seen afterwards, and your being put before a jury and being condemned to death. The end effect for you personally is exactly the same; under one procedure you're as dead as you are going to be under the other. But your chances not to be executed are greater under a regime, under a system of justice in which the very concept of justice plays a certain role, however imperfect, however corrupt. And this is, I think, a very great difference. Or take the fate of intellectual dissenters in the Soviet Union. The existence of such dissenters is extremely hazardous. It is not only that they cannot publish, but their life, liberty, and pursuit of happiness is jeopardized. Under certain conditions this happens in America, too, for example to the people who were ostracized in the McCarthy era, who couldn't publish, who couldn't review this movie, produce this, and write, and so forth. But those were exceptions, dangerous exceptions in the direction of tyranny, which were remedied very quickly by the prevailing concept of justice. Those people have been reinstated and have become successful again and so forth. So, I would still say, while the effect under certain conditions may be the same, the qualitative distinction remains vital and really still constitutes the difference between tyranny and monarchy, or between a regime without justice and a regime where at least a concept of justice puts certain limitations on the actions of government. You see, the people who say that we live in an oppressive society that is really no different from a totalitarian society simply don't know what it means to live in a totalitarian society.

Student: What you are saying is that there is the idealist element here that all politics is evil and the realist is saying, yes, but in some politics there is more justice than in others.

HJM: You are entirely correct. There is a Utopian element in the judgment that all governments are bad, to hell with all governments, let's go back to nature where nobody has ever been but which is the Golden Age. Sure, if you live in this world, you are surrounded by evil. Some people say it was Eve who did it. Others say it was the class division of society. You know that it wasn't the apple on the tree that is responsible for original sin but the pair on the ground!

CHAPTER 6

Justice and Revolution

I want to discuss today what is really the core of the Aristotelian political philosophy—one might say not only the Aristotelian but of any political philosophy—and that is the problem of justice. When you debate the nature of a particular political system and the merits of institutional arrangements and political measures, implicitly, if not explicitly, you apply a standard of justice. In other words, your evaluation is intended not to be subjective—not in your own interest or what is in the interest of just another group—but the standard that you apply is the standard of justice. You ask yourself, is this law that the Senate passed today just? You apply an objective standard to this particular legislation.

Aristotle tries to illuminate the principle of justice by using two corrupt systems of government—oligarchy and democracy. Oligarchy is the rule of the wealthy, and the principle of justice appropriate to oligarchy is the possession of wealth. Those who are wealthy can have a larger share in political rights and the benefits of the state than those who are poor. On the other hand, the principle of justice appropriate to democracy is the exact opposite. That those who are of equal birth, who are born free—all of them without any distinctions—shall also have equal rights. Obviously the principle of justice here is equated with the principle of equality. And, of course, this is not only an Aristotelian but also a modern principle. Those who are equal ought to be treated equally. The question arises, of course, equal with regard to what? The oligarchy says those who are equal in wealth ought to be treated equally. Democracy says that those who are equal with regard to free birth shall be treated equally.

This section includes seminars from April 4, 11, and 18, 1972.

The basis of the oligarchic claim is that those with more responsibility for property have more to lose and, thus, are more attentive to political matters. Up to the middle of the nineteenth century in England and up to 1919 in Prussia, this was the principle upon which suffrage was based: that only property owners had a stake in the state—that they have a sense of responsibility. The implication was that since they are property owners and they have amassed wealth or have inherited wealth and have an interest and have been successful in administering that wealth beneficially to themselves, they have already proven the ability to manage the state. The beggar who is a failure in his own individual life—and I use beggar here in a metaphorical sense—cannot be entrusted with political office and political responsibility, for the fact that he has failed in his individual life creates the presumption that he is going to fail on the political level as well. So the wealthy, the well-to-do (and the well-to-do has a dual connotation) doesn't only mean people who have done well economically but also those who have done well socially, who, in other words, have proven their worth, their ability to manage affairs. Therefore, they ought to have a proportionately higher share of public offices and public benefits. In Prussia you had the so-called three-class suffrage. In a descending scale you had cumulative votes according to the amount of property you had. If you look at aristocratic government in England, for instance, the men of means by definition were the natural rulers of the state because, first of all, they had a stake in the state because of their wealth, and secondly, they had proven their merit.

For those who inherited their wealth, this same logic would apply depending on their behavior. If they go through it in no time, they will be beggars and thereby lose their political privilege, but if they can keep their wealth and even increase it, they have proven that they are good people. Take the Rockefellers. Born rulers. And they believe it, too.

One might also note that the practice of administering the land trains one to rule. And so it follows logically that since they are trained in administering their land and they have those invisible emotional ties to the land, that they care about the piece of property for which they are responsible. You expand this territory to the territory of the state and you deal not with one landowner but with landowners collectively and you have the natural ruling class.

Student: But the wealthy few will rule in their own interest . . . ?

HJM: This is exactly the point that Aristotle raises: Is it just that a wealthy minority rules over the poor majority?

Student: Many people have the tendency to equate wealth with wisdom, and they are two entirely different things.

HJM: I don't move in circles where those two things are equated. What would happen to those people who have no wealth, like myself; they are devoid of wisdom. (Laughter) People with such opinions I don't talk to.

Student: When most people talk, they say the majority isn't too wise—the majority is mediocre, and they say that is why an elite should rule. The alternative is not an elite of intelligence, but just an elite of wealth. Just people that are wealthy, not people who are wise. And those rich people will rule in their own interest. It is confusion, I think, in the minds of many that they consider wealth synonymous with wisdom.

HJM: I doubt that most people go so far. And I don't think it is an argument that has to be taken seriously. But the other one certainly should be taken seriously because it has had an enormous influence upon the theory and practice of government.

Student: People who are elected to government who already have wealth may be perceived by the voters to be more honest than those who don't.

HJM: This is correct. This is a very serious argument, that the corruption that is concomitant with politics in our society is limited to people who need money. The millionaire who aspires to public office and gets it is immune to this kind of corruption. With this goes a kind of *noblesse oblige*, which is common among people who don't need to cater to what Theodore Roosevelt calls the malefactors of great wealth; not being exposed to the favors or the reprisals of pressure groups is a great asset in a public servant. In this respect there can't be any doubt that the possession of wealth is a positive factor when it comes to the issue of justice.

The argument I am making is not the question of wisdom connected with wealth, but rather the question of virtue, in the political sense, in the public sense, that the owner of wealth has a stake in the country because he has a stake in however small a part of the country. The man who doesn't own land in Athens is more liable to go to Corinth or to Sparta since he has no ties. He takes the next ship and goes, perhaps taking citizenship in another country. If he has a piece of land in Athens, he has a tie that creates certain values within his psyche that the landless individual, who is capable of migrating very easily, does not have. Anybody who has ever owned property, real property, is aware of the psychological effects that ownership of property has. If you own a house somewhere, you have a tie to this particular place and through it to the whole country, which you don't have if you rent a place to live.

Now if you turn from the principle of justice in an oligarchy to the principle of justice in a democracy, you get into another kind of difficulty: There is no reason why the people who happen to be born free should all be equally treated when it comes to the distribution of offices or the distribution of benefits in the public realm. Logically, the more accurate principle of justice is that those who are equal in a politically relevant sense—such as the ability to govern—ought to be dealt with equally. In other words, those who contribute equally to the common good— that is to say, the state—ought to be treated equally.

This is, I think, an unexceptional principle, but Aristotle is fully aware of the enormous difficulties that you face when you try to translate this principle into practice. What does it mean in practical terms when you say that all those who contribute equally to the common good ought to be treated equally? How do we determine who contributes to the public? And in what measure? That is the real problem. Certainly one can argue persuasively that the wealthy don't contribute equally to the common good because they are wealthy; but of course the argument has been made that they do so because they pay taxes and the poor don't pay taxes. So that the ones who pay taxes, or the amount of taxes they pay—the amount of real property they own—ought to be the determinant of their rewards because they contribute proportionately to the common good in the economic sense. But obviously the economic contribution is only one among a number of contributions that the individual can make to the common good. Take, for instance, the rendering of public services. Should members of the Peace Corps, civil servants, and members of the armed forces be singled out for special benefits because they make a special contribution to the public good?

One might argue that the sum total of private interests determines the objective common good. But there is really no objective standard because how do you determine the sum total of private interests—it is an abstraction that is impossible to define. Private interests are, of course, contradictory. And this is the stuff of which social and political and economic conflicts are made. If the private interests were running on parallel identical lines, you wouldn't have any problem, but the problem arises exactly because of the contradictory demands different groups make upon the public authorities. *Federalist Paper 51* is one of the Holy Scriptures for American pluralism.[1] It suggests that there is no objective principle of justice. The principle of justice is simply who gets what when. And what the justice amounts to is the conflict of pressure groups and who is more successful than the other—or the pressure group that is more successful than the other happens to justify its success by saying that this is justice. The pluralistic principle completely dissolves the concept of justice into a warring conglomeration of pressure groups; and which one is going to win is not a question of any objective standard, but of the distribution of power in society.

This is not to say that the American political tradition has no standard of objective justice. You wouldn't say that either *Federalist Paper 51* or the pressure groups of political thought are the only principles by which the American polity has oriented itself. Take the problem of slavery, particularly Lincoln's argument against slavery. Both Douglas and Lincoln tried to interpret the Declaration of Independence that all men are created equal.[2] But what does it mean? Douglas said it means white men, men who have descended from the British. Lincoln said it means all men, regardless of color, regardless of descent. And he makes the point that if you limit the principle of equality to white men descended from the British, in 1858 half of the American population is excluded from equality because they

---

1. In *Federalist Paper 51*, James Madison lays out the classic argument for a balance among the branches of government and the competing interests within a society. Morgenthau takes this argument further by arguing that it presumes there is no objective standard of justice, a rather unique interpretation of this piece.
2. Stephen Douglas (1813–1861) served as both a U.S. representative and a senator from Illinois. In 1858, as the incumbent Democrat for the Illinois Senate seat, he debated Abraham Lincoln in a series of debates that became famous throughout the nation for their focus on slavery and the status of the Union. While he defeated Lincoln for the Senate seat in 1858, Douglas lost in his bid for the presidency in 1860.

are not descended from the British, that is, they are immigrants. Of course, the percentage would become much greater in later years. So the pressure groups theory is correct as far as it goes, but it completely overlooks the moral framework within which it operates.

What then is equality? Is it based on equality of skills or equality at a different level? Some confuse equality with meritocracy, in the sense of a political and social conformism, what we call teamwork. I remember about ten years ago an employee of the Foreign Aid Mission in Laos discovered enormous fraud on the part of the construction companies, deficient work and corruption between the members of the Mission and the construction companies and so forth—and he reported it to Washington. He was shipped home first because he was not a team worker and, second, he was declared insane because if you don't play the game you must be out of your mind.

In fact, what we have both in the United States and the Soviet Union is really a conformism that imposes its values upon the members of a certain group, and members of that group either tow the line as it is prescribed by the social group or they are expelled from the social group. I will give you another example from my experience. I was for a few years a member of the faculty of a minor institution of higher learning that had a president who was a psychopathic crook (laughter) and who was not smart enough not to take a leave of absence for one year. The vice president who became the acting president discovered a great number of irregularities and he informed the Board of Trustees, whereupon the Board of Trustees fired the president because he was a crook—and they fired the vice president because he was disloyal to the president!

This is not what is generally called meritocracy. It is the manifestation of a national quality, conformism. And American conformism, which is an enormously strong force, performs a vital function for society because it keeps American society together. For American society is not based, like other societies, upon ethnic identity or dynastic identity or religious identity; rather it is based upon geographic proximity, but only in a very broad sense. More basically, it is based upon a psychologically social coherence that is in a sense spontaneous. Most of us have become American by an act of will. People have migrated to America, like I did, and it was an act of will by which we became Americans—which is a very tenuous, a very precarious integrated principle. So this enormously strong, enforced conformism is the cement that keeps American society together. It is a substitute for the traditional objective integrated factors that are present in other societies.

But this is not meritocracy. This is the spontaneous imposition of unorganized society of certain patterns of conduct that are accepted by the population at large. Take a political issue such as the war in Vietnam, and the public attitude toward it. And I speak here again from personal experience. The argument that I have encountered ten years ago, eight years ago, in my opposition to the war in Vietnam has been primarily the question: Who are you to put your judgment against the judgment of the president of the United States? How can you step out of line and act as if you had the wisdom and the virtue that the president of the United States has? So there is, however untenable this argument may be on rational grounds, a mechanical argument that is intended to force you into line. It doesn't make any difference whether the policy of the president is good or bad, wise or unwise, you don't step out of line. You march behind them. You have it very recently in the arguments of the present incumbent of the presidency [Richard Nixon] against his critics. And these are exactly the same arguments Mr. Johnson used to address to his critics. I remember when Robert Kennedy argued against the war in Vietnam in the Senate, I think in 1966, Mr. Johnson raised the question whether Mr. Kennedy was on the side of the president of the United States or on the side of Ho Chi Minh. It is the issue of where you belong, to what society you belong, where your loyalties lie. And the merits of the question, the merits of the issue are really secondary if they are discussed at all.

This tendency toward a spontaneously enforced conformity, enforced by unorganized society in America and imposed by totalitarian means (especially by terror and, of course, all persuasiveness of benefits) in the Soviet Union, has the same aim in both countries: to create and maintain a society that is—for different reasons in the United States and in the Soviet Union—extremely fragile.

Student: In regard to justice in a pluralistic society, it seems to me that Aristotle's concept compared to Plato's is one of a pluralistic nature.

HJM: No, you can't really say that because Aristotle's argument is very simple. It is the Machiavellian argument that "might makes right." You may also say that this is a relativistic pressure group argument, that there is no objective common group, and that the most you can say empirically is that whichever pressure group is capable of making its will prevail thereby defines the standards of justice, for the time being, until it is replaced by another pressure group. But certainly Aristotle was opposed to this.

What is interesting in Aristotle, and particularly for the problems of American democracy, is that he gives to the people at large—that is to say, to the democratic principles of justice—an advantage over the aristocratic principle, which accepts the standard of wealth as the determining factor. For he says that while certainly a wise judge is superior to any random member of the populace in his wisdom, all citizens together may have a higher degree of justice than one single man or a small group. It is, of course, very much in conformity with the modern conception of democratic justice. *Vox populi, vox dei.* Or the Jeffersonian principle that truth will emerge from the free debate of the citizenry as a whole.

Student: Constitutionality . . .

HJM: Which is, of course, antidemocratic, a nondemocratic institution. And to which liberals have pointed, especially when there was a conservative government, and they will soon have an opportunity to point to it again. (Laughter) But as long as the Supreme Court is libertarian, that is to say, follows the election returns, as the saying has it, one doesn't object to the nondemocratic character of the Supreme Court. But the Supreme Court is clearly in its function a nondemocratic institution. And it has been so intended. Because the Founding

Fathers were infinitely more skeptical about the wisdom and virtue of the populace at large than was Aristotle. Of course, Aristotle dealt with a very limited type of citizenry—with a minority of the people who lived in Athens. But the Founding Fathers had rather a negative opinion of what they called the citizenry at large. They may have been created equal but let's be very careful when it comes to voting.

Student: I am not quite sure I agree with this concept of American performance in the political system. What role do you see Americans performing and playing in the ultimate questions of who will and will not disturb political power and so forth?

HJM: When it comes to the operations of the democratic process of electing public officials, conformism doesn't need to play this kind of stifling role when it comes to policy and opinion. But it can play that role, too. Take a place like Chicago. Conformism plays a great role there. If it comes to municipal elections in Chicago, certainly you can run against Mr. Daley, but Mr. Daley doesn't really care much about this and the man who runs against him doesn't have the slightest chance to be elected. Why? Because what we call the iron discipline of the political machine, the very concept of the political machine is, of course, very closely related to conformism, because if you know what is good for you, you are not going to buck the machine. This is an issue that comes very close to totalitarian practices.

I am personally acquainted with a situation on the South Side of Chicago, in Woodlawn, where there is the First Presbyterian Church, which is located in the midst of the black ghetto, and which was once a very high crime section—the highest crime section of Chicago.[3] The pastor of this Church, a Reverend Frei, tried to create an organization of the black poor that would take care of their own interests. There was a gang, the Black Stone Nation, which was transformed into a kind of civic group with social activities, economic activities, business, and so forth. This was a very interesting social experiment, but it was independent of the political powers of City Hall. It was an autonomous institution, and so City Hall tried to destroy this institution by means that I find quite appalling. For instance, the Reverend Frei was once driving his car and he was run off the street by a police car. The police officer got out and said, "If you don't get out of town, you will not live." There was a similar threat a second time, and the third time two police officers came to his house and asked for him in such a way that he went out the back door, put his family in the car, and left for California and never came back. Now this is also conformism of a particular kind, which is, I think, closely associated with the political machine, which is part and parcel of the concept of a political machine. Where political machines do not exist, again by definition, you have at least a certain degree, a high degree of political competition. And conformism plays no role in that.

---

3. There is a First Presbyterian Church in Woodlawn, Chicago, but I have not been able to verify the story that Morgenthau is recounting.

Student: In other words, you mean to say that you believe the American people, by nature, will have to be jarred to their senses much more strongly, and it will take much more time for them to be shaken from their conformism to depose their leaders than would be the case in Italy and France?

HJM: You can certainly say that when you look at the disengagement of France from Algeria and our inability to disengage ourselves from Indochina. Certainly a radical break with a particular policy or a particular ruling group in the United States always implies the risk of dissolution of society.

When a great debate evolved over slavery, it was solved not by a vote in Congress or by judicial decision but by civil war. Which is again an obvious manifestation of the fragility of American society as compared to other societies. In other words, we cannot afford the kind of radical changes in policy and in personnel of government because those changes—because of the fragility of our society—do not only imply what they are obviously aiming at, changes in policy or personnel, but they also imply a crisis of American society itself. But of course a living organism like a society shies away from such a test of its viability.[4]

I want to continue today the discussion we started last time—the problem of revolution.[5] And I want to remind you of the distinction Aristotle makes between two kinds of revolutions: one, a revolution that overthrows the constitution, that interrupts the constitutional continuity; and, two, a revolution that occurs within an existing and persisting constitutional framework. It is, of course, the latter type of revolution that gives rise to problems. When a people rise and overthrow a constitution like the French did in 1789, or when a military junta takes over the government and scraps the constitution, as has happened so many times all over the world, you have a simple, clear-cut case, while a revolution within the existing constitutional framework is obviously a very vague and ambiguous situation. You have an inkling of this ambiguity if you consider the many partisan movements all over the world that call themselves revolutionary and that imply a radical change in the distribution of political power within the existing constitutional framework. We speak, for instance, of the revolution of the New Deal, which only means that this so-called revolution has brought about drastic changes in the distribution of power within the existing constitutional framework. If somebody would say it was not a revolution but a radical reform, he would mean exactly the same thing. So one has to be careful when one talks about revolution. I think it would be wiser to use the term only for those political movements that actually interrupt, that actually sever the constitutional continuity.

Aristotle also raises the question as to whether or not all revolutions arise from the problem of equality, or, said differently, is the source of revolution always the

---

4. At this point in the transcription, the transcriber wrote, "Tape ran out before the end of the lecture." It would appear that Morgenthau pursued this line of discussion further into an analysis of revolution, based on the fact that the next seminar directly addresses this topic.
5. A seminar from April 11, 1972, begins here.

issue of justice. That is to say, a group of people within a state revolts either within the constitutional framework or by overthrowing it because it feels itself to be unjustly treated. So this is the basic revolutionary situation. A potent sector of the population experiences injustice in the form of inequality and in order to remedy this injustice it revolts.

Aristotle also distinguishes between the case of the revolution and the root case of the revolution, which is injustice in the form of inequality, and the occasion on which a revolution arises. Revolutions have arisen (again, Germany and Spain are examples) when a group of people who were subject to burdensome laws or were afraid of certain legal consequences instigated a revolution in order to escape them. Take the so-called Nazi revolution, which of course was a real revolution even though it started out within the constitutional framework of the Weimar Republic. How did the Nazis come to power? A committee of the parliament investigated the relationships between the government and the feudal barons in East Prussia, and they found gross irregularities. They found a little nest of corruption. And before the committee could submit its report, which would have been extremely damaging to that small group of aristocrats, those feudal barons prevailed upon Hindenburg, the president (who was close to senility at that time, and whose son was his aide-de-camp, a particularly stupid member of this group), to dissolve the Reichstag in order to prevent this report from being published. And the next elections brought about a distribution of votes that left Hindenburg only two choices: either make a dictatorship or make Hitler the chancellor of Germany.

In Spain you have a very similar situation. The laws of the Republic, aimed at the expropriation of the Catholic Church, were the final straw that brought about the counterrevolution, which had been planned long before and which was planned in close contact with the German propaganda and planning agencies. So you see, there are all kinds of revolution, and not only the revolutions that we have in mind when we think of the American or the French Revolution of 1789; there are revolutions from the Right and from the Left and from all sides. Whenever you have a group of citizens who feel either aggrieved or threatened to such an extent that they prefer the risk of civil war to the continuation of the constitutional status quo, we have a revolutionary situation.

Some might doubt that the Nazis coming to power constitute a revolution. But it did drastically alter social relations, thus making a revolution in the Aristotelian sense. For example, nobody had ever heard in Germany before 1933 of paid vacations for workers. Hundreds of thousands of workers were sent around all over Europe on vacations. Nobody had even dreamt of this before. Furthermore, full employment. I remember I came back to Germany in 1935 and I talked to a Catholic labor leader whom I had known before, and he said you have to give Hitler credit for the fact that he had abolished unemployment. And unemployment in Germany before 1933 did not mean what unemployment means here; it meant that if you had lost your job, you had lost it for good. You are finished as a useful human being. You can sell apples on the next street corner if somebody gives you credit for a couple of apples, but otherwise you are finished. So anybody who had lost his job before 1933 got his social and economic death sentence. Hitler saved the people from this predicament. Hitler wasn't so popular for nothing. We have a very simplified conception of fascism because we oppose it, but to oppose it doesn't mean you have to close your eyes to the enormous attraction, a genuine popular attraction fascism can have under certain conditions. If the conditions are right, there will be an attraction to fascism in any country—there is no country immune from the particular temptation that exists when a gross inequality persists without the slightest hope of remedy and somebody comes along and says, "Give me your freedom. I'll give you security and I'll give you a position within a splendid imperial hierarchy."

Student: This still doesn't constitute a revolution. It seems to me in Aristotle's terms this would be more like a degeneration of a mob, a bunch of gangsters, who took power and made it a revolution in the second sense.

HJM: But you see, the distinction between a group of gangsters and a respectable government is extremely tenuous. St. Augustine made this point—that a government is a bunch of robbers without justice. I mean, the people who govern us are just a little bit smarter, smart enough to stay on the right side of the law. Otherwise they would be Mafiosi, and the Mafiosi are just stupid enough or unlucky enough to remain on the wrong side of the law. But there are occasions, as we all know, where those two realms of government merge.

Student: If it comes to the point where the government rules illegitimately in the minds of most of the citizens and yet the army remains loyal, what do you see as the scenario?

HJM: We might also consider the extent to which these conditions exist in the United States today. I think the Vietnam War has certainly been a catalyst for many issues that have been present. The inability of the government to solve any of the major problems with which American society is faced, such as inflation, unemployment, race, the cities, is leading to a crisis situation. Wherever you look, unequal and oppressive taxation frequently has been the spur to revolution. You have a host of problems, none of which is being solved; and there isn't an expectation that they will be solved, which is really the important thing. What is important in such a situation is not only what actually exists, but what people perceive as the possibilities of the future.

For instance, what demoralized the Weimar Republic and brought about the polarization between the Communists and Nazis was exactly the utter hopelessness of the situation. It was not unemployment per se but it was the impossibility to visualize the existing constitutional framework and within the existent policies of the government any solution to the problems. The federal government was obsessed with the idea of the balanced budget. One of the few items in the budget that you could manipulate was social services, unemployment insurance and so forth. So you cut unemployment insurance in order to balance the budget. In consequence you cut, of course, the consumptive power of the masses of the people and you increase unemployment. And so your budget goes out of balance again. And so on and so on and you are in a vicious circle. The policy, for instance, of the Weimar government really amounted to slow starvation. Keynes was hardly known; I think there were one or two writers who suggested Keynsian remedies, and they were regarded as crackpots. So the balancing of the budget was the main issue for the government, which was, of course, a self-destructive policy in view of the economic issues that it faced. And so, while the people at large were unaware of the subtleties of economic theory, they were fully aware of the hopelessness of the situation; that with those policies you never will go back to employment. You will slowly starve to death. This was not true of just a couple of hundred thousand, but I think at the height of the unemployment there were 6 million unemployed— 10 percent of the population. I remember well in 1932 scores of people telling me in Germany that this government can't do it, give Hitler a chance. If Hitler promises he can do it, are we going to starve to death in order to prove that he can't do it?

In other words, it is not a question of theory, it is a question of the immediate experiences of people who simply are driven to desperation. You had this issue among French historians of the French Revolution. The main school of thought has always held that the French Revolution broke out because of the ideas of the Enlightenment of the eighteenth century. That people were possessed with the spirit of liberty and so forth and manned the barricades and the leader of the other school, Faguet, said, "They didn't want to starve to death."[6] And when you are faced with starving to death you are very likely to make revolution. So you see, revolution is not something that is figured out by doctrinaires—it may be figured out by doctrinaires—but is put in practice by desperate people. Why did the Bol-shevists win in October 1917 and not Kerensky? Not because the Russian people didn't want to starve to death but they didn't want to be killed anymore for noth-ing. There was also famine, of course, but the main point was peace. Lenin's suc-cess was a result of his understanding of the basic popular aspiration in Russia, which was to make an end to the war—peace.

Student: If the German government of the interwar period was democratic, why did people fall for Hitler?

HJM: First of all, the republic was born out of the defeat of Germany, and the defeat was experienced in Germany as a completely unforeseen event. The Ger-man armies were everywhere in enemy country, and all of a sudden in October 1918, Ludendorff, the great genius of the German army, asked for an armistice, and everybody said, "What is going on?" It's like Nixon going on television to-night and saying, "We surrender to the Soviet Union and we will receive Mr. Pod-gorny as the new president of the United States tomorrow." People would say, "What's going on? What is this?" Here victorious Germany, having suffered enor-mous losses that were incomparably greater in terms of the armed forces than they were in the Second World War, all of a sudden finds itself defeated with all of its armies in enemy territory. So people ask, "What's going on?" And then the old regime invented the myth of the stab in the back. Our victorious armies were

---

6. Emile Faguet (1847–1916) was a French literary critic who wrote essays on the French Revolution in the context of French intellectual history.

stabbed in the back by the domestic enemies—the Marxists, the Jews, the Catholics, the Free Masons—and that is the beginning of Nazism. This was, you may say, the root cause of Nazism.

Hitler and ten other veterans of the First World War got together in 1919 and said, "This will not happen in Germany again. And the first thing we need to do is to cleanse Germany of its domestic enemies." At the same time the Kaiser had fled, the whole government had dissolved, and somebody had to take over. As I told you, the Socialist leader went to the balcony and declared a republic. So the stigma of betrayal, the stigma of defeat was attached to the republic; because it first coincided with the defeat, millions of people believed that the defeat was a result of the republic—that the republic had betrayed Germany and "sold it down the river."

Then came the second shock—inflation. Now, when we talk about inflation today in this country, we talk about something quite disagreeable; but when you talk about inflation between 1920 and 1923 in Germany, you are talking about a catastrophe of absolutely unimaginable proportions. In the fall of 1923, one gold mark was worth one billion marks in paper money. I have still some billion-paper marks in a folder. I remember when my mother went to the market with a basket full of paper marks. The result was that all decent people who had put their money in savings bonds or in savings accounts and so forth were completely wiped out. There weren't any billionaires in Germany, and if there had been anybody who had a decent fortune with a couple of hundred thousand marks now had 50 cents in 1923. He had nothing. He was finished. What does it mean? It meant they were beggars. There was no social security or anything; they had nothing. On the other hand, the crooks who understood the mechanics of inflation would borrow and buy anything—houses, shoes, livestock, mountains (laughter)—whatever you could buy. They bought to get rid of the paper money, and six months later they paid back the loan in devaluated currency.

I remember I was in 1923 a freshman at the University of Frankfurt. There was a branch of the bank on the access road to the university. Every student in the morning went in there, got rid of the two or three marks he had in his pocket and bought some stock or whatever it was because if you walked around with two marks in your pocket in the morning, in the afternoon it was worth one mark and 50 cents. And at the end of the week it was worth 10 cents. So you got rid of the stuff as soon as you could. My father was a doctor and got as fees a pound of butter, a piece of linen, some leather for shoes, anything—but no money because money just dissolved in your hands. The result of this was, of course, the destruction of the German middle class; the objective "proletarization" of the middle classes with a very interesting un-Marxist result in that the pauperized middle classes revolted against the proletarization and became fascist.

And then you had unemployment. The Nazis explained all these catastrophes, one following the other, as the result of a Jewish Marxist conspiracy out to destroy the German people. If you experience this and you get this drummed into you day in and day out, it is bound to make an impression on you. Could you have maintained a democratic government? You could have maintained a pseudo-constitutional government in the form of a military dictatorship within the constitutional framework continuing to govern as it did before under Article 48 of the Constitution, that is to say, the emergency provision. But what was decisive was not the kind of government you had in constitutional terms, but what kind of policy the government would pursue. As long as you had a government that couldn't think of anything else but a balanced budget, I mean the strict form of Republican conception in this country, this led to the continuing and ever-aggravated ruin of Germany. It couldn't be otherwise.

Could discontent over Vietnam lead to a similar revolution in the United States today? Vietnam is fortunately a marginal enterprise within the overall context of United States policy and psychology. What you had in Germany is something entirely different. A whole generation was wiped out. There was hardly a family of which not a member was killed in the war. So you had a devastation that is just shocking. I was brought up in a small town in Germany where I knew hundreds of families. How many only sons of these families had been killed? And I remember when the Nazis became strong in the 1930s, the widows or the mothers without their sons looking at my mother and me with real hatred. Why is that guy alive and my son dead? Americans have no conception of the moral devastation that the First World War wrought in Germany. All for nothing. We are already afraid of making peace in Vietnam because we say 50,000 men have died for nothing. That is bad enough. But here I forget now, I think 3 million Germans were killed in the First World War. This, one shouldn't forget, is an enormous lasting wound in the body polity; and to give meaning to this so far meaningless sacrifice became an obsession of millions of people whose life got a new meaning because they said, "Now we have somebody who is going to avenge our sons and husbands." We in America have experienced this on a much smaller scale and within a political and social system that has an expectation of success and has lots of success to its credit. So you have an entirely different situation from that which existed in Germany at the time.

Student: This experience has obviously affected you—can you tell us how much difference it has made in your life?

HJM: Obviously I can't tell you how much. It certainly has affected it. I have experienced it. And obviously I haven't come down from heaven to this chair and started to teach. I mean, obviously my mind has been formed by certain experiences. And naturally those experiences are part of my intellectual composition.

I want to discuss this evening the distinctions that Aristotle makes with regard to three basic issues connected with revolution.[7] First, what are the psychological motives of revolution? Second, what are the objects of revolution? And third, what are the occasions out of which revolutions arise?

---

7. A seminar from April 18, 1972, begins here.

As far as the psychological motives are concerned, we have to go back to the fundamental principles that form the whole of politics, that is, the principle of justice. Men want justice and out of the unsatisfied aspiration for justice revolutions arise. The nature of revolution is always the realization of justice.

As we know, justice according to Aristotle is identical with equality. And here you have two different motives for revolution—according to whether a revolution takes place in a democracy or in an oligarchy, or I should rather say whether it is a democratic or an oligarchic revolution. That is to say, a democratic revolution is one that tries to increase the degree of equality in society; people who are equal or regard themselves to be equal in certain respects have an innate tendency to become equal in every respect. So there is a tendency inherent in a democratic mode of thinking to exaggerate the principle of equality; and since inequality to a certain degree is always present in society, there exists a tendency toward revolution that wants to bring about complete equality.

On the other hand, oligarchy is based upon the principle of inequality. People are unequal in certain respects. The aristocracy governs by virtue of heredity or belonging to a particular group of people. The king in a monarchy governs by the grace of God. This is an extreme case of inequality. That is to say, there is only one man in the whole society who has a right to govern because only he governs by the charisma of divine grace. This being so, those people who are set apart in certain respects, who govern by the principle of inequality, have again a tendency to overdo it, to exaggerate the principle of inequality by assuming the people who are in certain respects unequal are unequal in every respect. And though you have a tendency toward extremism (as we would say today) in favor either of equality or of inequality, the disturbances of the status quo and of constitutional continuity are the result of those two extreme aspirations or those aspirations towards extremes, either equality or inequality. A democratic revolution is an attempt to realize absolute equality, and an oligarchic or aristocratic revolution is the attempt to realize complete inequality. So much for the psychological motives of a revolution. They are always the result of an experienced dissatisfaction with a degree of justice achieved, and justice can be defined either in terms of equality or of inequality.

Student: When Aristotle uses the word aristocracy, he is referring to a class. He is not using the word in the same sense as it is used in terms of national aristocracy.

HJM: You cannot exclude this altogether because aristocracy in the Aristotelian sense is a meritocracy, or a group of people who excel in certain respects, who stick out among the mass. Of course, the difficult case is the case of hereditary aristocracy. But it isn't necessarily so.

Student: But in this sense, if Aristotle made the assumption that merit was something that was genetically transmitted, then it seems to me that he was a step behind Plato.

HJM: This is what Aristotle would assume, too. He distinguishes types of aristocratic rule, and certainly the aristocratic families are a typical and easily identifiable group who govern in the aristocratic manner. But it is quite possible to have an educational aristocracy, and Aristotle makes a point that education is a prerequisite for any kind of sound rule. But where education is limited to an aristocracy, to a particular group of people, you have an aristocratic type of government. Where education is spread to large masses of the people, you have a polity, or, what we would say, an intelligent, rational educated democracy. So the concept of aristocracy does not refer as, let me say, European writers might imply, or the European tradition would imply, to an aristocracy by birth. That is only one particular type of aristocracy. It may well be an oligarchy if this particular aristocracy by birth really doesn't merit to rule because it doesn't contribute to the common good. If it uses its privileged position for its own benefit, rather than for the common good, it becomes an oligarchy. It is a corrupt aristocracy.

Student: From my interpretation of the comparison of Plato and Aristotle, it seems to me that Aristotle was much more conservative.

HJM: What do you mean by conservative?

Student: In terms of maintaining the status quo. Plato was more prone to advocate change.

HJM: Well, I would be dubious about that. Aristotle is, of course, in favor of a stable society—really a kind of middle-class society; and for this reason he had a considerable influence on the thinking of the Founding Fathers, either directly or through the intermediary of Locke.

Student: Didn't Plato reject the idea of a middle class?

HJM: Surely he rejected it. He was in favor of a much more rigid form of society in which an aristocracy, however appointed, and the philosopher king would rule without interference from the people at large. You see, both Plato and Aristotle were confronted with the decay of Athenian democracy, and both wanted to stop it. Both looked for a remedy by which the Athenian state could be saved. It is difficult for me to deal with modern concepts such as radicalism and conservatism when you deal with Plato and Aristotle. When in the 1930s some people had written books proving that fascism was a direct descendent from Plato—that was a very dubious kind of argument. Because it projects without qualifications (and the qualifications may well destroy the projections) modern ways of thinking into a kind of discourse that is entirely different. That has entirely different modes of thought and of judgment. It is much more so in the case of Plato than of Aristotle. For this reason we can really deal with Aristotle as a kind of modern thinker. And for this reason Aristotle has had such an enormous influence upon Western political thought. Plato has had an enormous influence upon philosophy, but not upon political philosophy. You can read Aristotle making allowances for certain obsolete archaic things but you can read him like a modern writer: a little bit discursive, but more easily understandable than the kind of modern political writers I had the misfortune to read.

Select Annotated Bibliography

Note: The following list is not intended to be a complete bibliography; recent publications on Morgenthau's life and works have provided us with such overviews. I have chosen instead to provide a short annotated bibliography of some of the most important works by Morgenthau and some of the secondary literature on him. I have left out some of Morgenthau's monographs and many of his articles, instead focusing on those that relate to the seminars on Aristotle. Works on Morgenthau continue to be produced. I have included only those works I drew upon in preparing the manuscript of these seminars.

WORKS BY HANS J. MORGENTHAU (arranged chronologically)

Books

Scientific Man vs. Power Politics (Chicago: University of Chicago Press, 1946; Midway reprint, 1974).

> In this book, Morgenthau critiques positivist social science just as it was becoming the norm in the social sciences and political science more specifically. This book has received mixed reviews, with some arguing it is one of the more devastating critiques of overly scientific forms of analysis while others argue it does not fairly characterize the positivist method. Morgenthau's years at the University of Chicago put him in the midst of a heated debate between supporters of positivist approaches, such as Charles Merriam and Harold Lasswell, and opponents of that approach, led by Leo Strauss (who arrived at the University of Chicago in 1949).

Politics among Nations: The Struggle for Power and Peace (New York: Alfred A. Knopf Publishers, 1948).

This book is the one that made Morgenthau famous in the field of international affairs. Morgenthau saw it as an introductory textbook to international affairs, but had trouble marketing it as such. It was eventually published by Knopf and went on to be published in six different editions. The six principles of political realism were added in the second edition (1954) in response to Morgenthau's critics. Other editions were published in1960 (3rd), 1967 (4th), 1973 (5th), and 1986 (6th). The last edition was published after Morgenthau's death in 1981, with some minor revisions by Kenneth Thompson, his student and longtime collaborator on *Politics among Nations*. An abridged version was published in 1993 as well.

In Defense of the National Interest (New York: Alfred A. Knopf, 1951).

This work was an important contribution to the debates about U.S. foreign policy as it emerged from World War II and sought to develop its policies toward the Soviet Union. Morgenthau argued that the national interest should be the lodestar to guide U.S. foreign policy, seeking a middle ground between excessive idealism and pure *realpolitik*. He uses the history of U.S. foreign policy to locate the national interest in a parallel fashion to George Kennan's *American Diplomacy, 1900–1950*.

Politics in the Twentieth Century: Dilemmas of Politics (Chicago: University of Chicago Press, 1958): volume 1, *The Decline of Democratic Politics*; volume 2, *The Impasse of American Foreign Policy* (1962); volume 3, *The Restoration of American Politics* (1962).

This three-volume collection of Morgenthau's essays, reviews, and short talks presents a wide-ranging study of his thought. The works were loosely organized by Morgenthau to demonstrate a decline in American politics, how it influenced foreign policy, and the possibilities for a revival. The essays cover too many topics to be covered here, but the entire collection is highly recommended not only for understanding Morgenthau but also because of the contributions it makes to perennial political problems.

The Purpose of American Politics (New York: Alfred A. Knopf, 1960).

This book presents one of Morgenthau's most important, and unnoticed, contributions to the study of international affairs: the idea of the national purpose. This concept is that which gives meaning and normative purpose to foreign policy. For the United States, that purpose is the combination of equality and freedom. Not all states have a national purpose, according to Morgenthau, which can help explain why not all states have an effective and influential presence on the world stage.

Truth and Power: Essays of Decade, 1960–1970 (New York: Praeger Publishers, 1970).

The essays contained in this volume present Morgenthau in a role he adopted in the latter part of his writings—the prophet speaking "truth to power." They focus on various individuals and decisions in U.S. foreign policy. His opposition to the Vietnam War is also expressed in many of these pieces, especially those focused on the Johnson administration.

Articles

"The Evil of Politics and the Ethics of Evil," *Ethics* 56, no. 1 (October 1945): 1–18.

> This article, written at the end of World War II, does not mention the Nazis or the Soviets, what one might expect from Morgenthau writing at this moment. Instead, he argues that the failure to understand the difference between ethics and politics leads to assumptions about good and evil that cannot be sustained in a world where humans pursue power. One sentence stands out: "Political ethics is indeed the ethics of doing evil."

"Views of Nuremberg: Further Analysis of the Trial and Its Importance," *America* (December 7, 1946): 266–267.

> This short piece, published in the Jesuit magazine, *America*, criticized the Nuremberg trials as winners' justice. He mentions this article in the Aristotle seminars, as late as 1970, so it does not appear that he came to doubt this position.

"Another Great Debate: The National Interest of the United States," *American Political Science Review* 46, no. 4 (December 1952): 961–988.

> In this article, Morgenthau aggressively takes on the critics of his book, *In Defense of the National Interest*, along with critics of Kennan's book, *American Diplomacy, 1900–1950*. He claims that the critics are not simply disagreeing with his views on foreign policy, but have a radically different concept of the human person and politics—a theme that would run through the rest of his works, including the seminars on Aristotle.

"Thought and Action in Politics," *Social Research* 38, no. 4 (winter 1971); reprinted in *Social Research* 51 (spring 1984): 143–165.

> In this short article, Morgenthau draws upon Aristotle and Plato extensively to examine what is the relationship between thought and action. He poses the ancient contrast between the "man of thought" and the "man of action," claiming that the former provides less help to the latter than the former imagines. He argues that the fully human person finds a place of tension between action and thought—an almost direct mirror of Aristotle's notion of what constitutes the fully realized human person.

"Human Rights and Foreign Policy" (First Distinguished CRIA Lecture on Morality and Foreign Policy, Council on Religion and International Affairs, New York, 1979).

> This lecture was given by Morgenthau in 1978 and was followed by a symposium with a number of invited participants. The lecture and symposium provide an important insight into Morgenthau's views on human rights. When pushed in the discussion, he moves to a theological defense of human rights, a surprising move in light of the lack of discussion of religious themes in his earlier work. This lecture is now considered the first CRIA lecture, which in 1986 became the Carnegie Council on Ethics and International Affairs, Morgenthau Lectures on Foreign Policy, which continue to this day.

"The Pathology of American Power," *International Security* 3 (winter 1977): 3–20.

> In this article, Morgenthau examines the failure of American foreign policy in the
> late 1970s, an earlier version of the "declinist" thesis made popular in the 1980s,
> but with more philosophical grounding. He uses nuclear weapons as a symbol of
> what is wrong with American policy in the later 1970s, arguing that it limits diplo-
> macy, makes negotiation impossible, and eliminates the potential for rational politi-
> cal action. He also uses this occasion to lambaste détente as a foreign policy used to
> rationalize actions that have no justification. He also concludes this piece with the
> failure of the United States to help resolve world poverty.

WORKS ABOUT HANS J. MORGENTHAU

Books

Kenneth J. Thompson and Robert J. Myers, eds., *Truth and Tragedy: A Tribute to Hans J.
Morgenthau*, 2nd, augmented edition (New Brunswick, NJ: Transaction Publishers,
1984 [1976]).

> This book is an edited collection of papers by his former students and a few other in-
> vited contributors. The essays use Morgenthau to explore various important issues
> in philosophy and international relations. The book includes two important works
> by Morgenthau: "Fragment of an Intellectual Autobiography, 1904–1932," which
> gives some interesting insights into Morgenthau's upbringing; and an interview
> Morgenthau gave later in his life. The editors note that the essays were to have in-
> cluded a piece by Hannah Arendt but she died before she could contribute anything.
> Those who did contribute reflect a wide divergence of thought: Robert Osgood,
> Louis Halle, Richard Falk, George Liska, Herbert Butterfield, and Adam Watson.

Michael J. Smith, *Realist Thought from Weber to Kissinger* (Baton Rouge: Louisiana State
University Press, 1986).

> In one of the best works that links together various realist thinkers, Smith locates
> Morgenthau along with E. H. Carr, Reinhold Niebuhr, George Kennan and Henry
> Kissinger. His account of Morgenthau is more critical than most, though, conclud-
> ing that his ideas of the national interest lack enough clarity to truly serve as a mode
> of political action.

Greg Russell, *Hans J. Morgenthau and the Ethics of American Statecraft* (Baton Rouge:
Louisiana State University Press, 1990).

> The first book to focus solely on Morgenthau, this volume explores the ways in
> which Morgenthau understood the American political project. Russell weaves to-
> gether a wide range of sources to demonstrate the effects on Morgenthau of the
> diverse strands that compose the philosophy of U.S. foreign policy. He also demon-
> strates how Morgenthau's writing helped shape that tradition, contributing to an
> "American realist tradition."

Joel Rosenthal, *Righteous Realists: Political Realism, Responsible Power, and American
Culture in the Nuclear Age* (Baton Rouge: Louisiana State University Press, 1991).

An intellectual history of American realism, this work locates Morgenthau in a larger body of thought, including Reinhold Niebuhr, George Kennan, Walter Lippmann and Henry Kissinger. Rosenthal argues that this approach to world affairs sought to find a "responsible" use of American power, especially in the nuclear age. This book usefully positions Morgenthau's thoughts on nuclear power with responsibility and politics.

Christoph Frei, *Hans J. Morgenthau: An Intellectual Biography* (Baton Rouge: Louisiana State University Press, 2001).

This work, written by an author fluent in the languages in which Morgenthau wrote (English, German, Spanish, French) provides important insights into his early, European period. It was published in German in 1994 and only later translated into English. Drawing on diaries and unpublished papers provided by Morgenthau's children, Frei makes the case that one of the most important influences upon Morgenthau was Friedrich Nietzsche. This influence can be seen in Morgenthau's interest in power. Comparing Frei's account with the seminars on Aristotle (which Frei also read) demonstrates the wide range of influences on Morgenthau's thoughts and ideas. The book contains a chronological bibliography of Morgenthau's works, in multiple languages.

M. Benjamin Mollov, *Power and Transcendence: Hans J. Morgenthau and the Jewish Experience* (Lanham, MD: Lexington Books, 2002).

This book provides yet another important insight into the sources of Morgenthau's thoughts. Mollov focuses on the importance of Morgenthau's religious background, especially as it relates to his views on human rights and ethics. Mollov also highlights the fact that Morgenthau supported the work of many American Jewish groups, especially those dedicated to helping Russian Jewry escape from the Soviet Union. This book contains an extensive bibliography.

Richard Ned Lebow, *The Tragic Vision of Politics: Ethics, Interests, and Orders* (Cambridge: Cambridge University Press, 2003).

This book, by one of Morgenthau's last students, locates Morgenthau in relation to Clausewitz and Thucydides. Rather than explore how they all reflect the same truths about international relations, Lebow skillfully examines the nexus of politics and ethics. Lebow's analysis of Morgenthau in this book situates him more firmly in a tradition focused on the ethical dilemmas that international politics presents.

Articles

Robert Jervis, "Hans Morgenthau, Realism, and the Scientific Study of International Politics," *Social Research* 61, no. 4 (1994): 853–876.

This article, by a leading scholar of foreign policy theory, points to the ethical dimensions of Morgenthau's work. At the same time, it notes that Morgenthau saw a tension between ethical rules and the demands of politics. This article also compares Morgenthau with the vogue of "science" in the study of international affairs, of which Jervis is a leading proponent.

A.J.H. Murray, "The Moral Politics of Hans Morgenthau," *Review of Politics* 58, no. 1 (1996): 81–107.

This article presents Morgenthau in terms of his focus on ethics. Disputing the works by Rosenthal and Russell as too American in their orientation, Murray suggests that Morgenthau was exploring ethical dilemmas from the classical tradition, that is, Aristotle and Plato. This article is important for locating Morgenthau's ethical reflections in a non-American setting.

Index

About the Editor

ANTHONY F. LANG, JR. is Lecturer in the School of International Relations at the University of St. Andrews. He has been Assistant Professor in departments of Political Science at the American University in Cairo and Albright College. He has also served as program officer at the Carnegie Council on Ethics and International Affairs in New York City.

www.ingramcontent.com/pod-product-compliance
Lightning Source LLC
Chambersburg PA
CBHW070243290326
41929CB00046B/2439